TRAILS OF TEARS
PATHS OF BEAUTY

The Story of the Navajos
and the Cherokees

TRAILS OF TEARS
PATHS OF BEAUTY

JOSEPH BRUCHAC

NATIONAL
GEOGRAPHIC

WASHINGTON, D.C.

Followed by a line of struggling Indian porters, a party of Spanish conquistadores pushes through the dense forest of the Southeast in search of gold and silver. Instead of riches, they encountered the fierce resistance of the Cherokees.

PAGE 1: A sandpainting takes shape by the hand of Navajo artist Eugene B. Joe.

PRECEDING PAGES: Late afternoon light strikes a butte on the Navajo Reservation near Window Rock, Arizona, about three miles south of Fort Defiance, the starting point for the Navajos' Long Walk.

CONTENTS

COPYRIGHT NOTICE AND LIBRARY OF CONGRESS
CIP DATA APPEAR ON PAGE 200.

AN OVERVIEW OF CHEROKEE HISTORY MAKES

us wonder that there are any Cherokees left alive, much less any organized Cherokee governments or identifiable Cherokee culture. Yet we are here. In fact, we seem to be everywhere.

Today there are three federally recognized Cherokee "tribes": the Cherokee Nation and the United Keetoowah Band, both with headquarters in Tahlequah, Oklahoma, and the Eastern Band of Cherokees in North Carolina. There are tribes with state recognition and at least 30 other groups calling themselves Cherokee. Thousands of individuals identify themselves as Cherokee without any group affiliation.

What does all this tell us? First of all, that we are a resilient, determined people. A further look tells even more. The current Cherokee population is incredibly diverse, ranging from full-blood, bilingual people to blond, blue-eyed people with fractions of Cherokee blood and no ties to any traditional Cherokee community. Many have nothing in common beyond their pride in being Cherokee and their determination to declare it to the world.

And what about cultural survival? Within the Cherokee population, there is a core group of perhaps 10,000 full-blood Cherokee speakers living in scattered Cherokee communities. They participate in traditional stomp dances or attend Cherokee churches (usually Baptist) making use of Cherokee language Bibles and hymn books. They engage in activities which are part of Cherokee culture: food gathering, craftmaking, community meetings, and the untranslatable *gadugi,* where people get together to help a neighbor in need.

They are involved in cultural preservation without being aware of it. They simply live the way they live. From this core group, the rings move out in all directions, as when a pebble is thrown into a body of water, wider ripples growing fainter—yet Cherokee all the same.

ROBERT CONLEY
Cherokee Author

MOST NAVAJOS LIVING TODAY ARE FOUR OR FIVE

generations away from ancestors who made the Long Walk. My own grand-father was six years old when he made the journey and ten when he returned from it. I was five when he died in 1948, but I still remember him singing and bouncing me on his knee. In my growing years, I heard his stories through my family. He told of always running, hiding, and being hungry.

In the summer of 1863, his starving band came across a patch of corn and squash in the Chuska Mountains. They were cooking when American soldiers and Ute scouts attacked them. My grandfather became separated from his family in the confusion, and he hid in a thick juniper tree. Through the dust and smoke, he heard screams of women and children shot down as they tried to run for cover. He survived the incident and subsisted on berries, piñon nuts, and yucca fruit for many days before being captured.

The Long Walk and Bosque Redondo represent a dark period in Navajo history. Driven to desperation by inhuman treatment, poverty, and hunger, the people committed many acts that violated traditional laws and customs. My grandfather talked of the stealing or fighting over food rations and of American soldiers carrying loaves of bread into the camps and asking for young women. "We committed every violation there," he used to say. With over half the captives dying, many traditional ceremonies were lost and many clans and family histories came to an end. It was also a time of great hero-ism of Navajo leaders who stood up against the U.S. government to demand fair treatment for their people and a return to their homeland.

In the year 2000, the Navajos number over 300,000 people and have managed to triple the size of the treaty reservation to 25,000 square miles. We have our own tribal government with an infrastructure that can match most state governments, our own college, and legislators in New Mexico and Arizona. Our votes have been a deciding factor in several Arizona elections.

We've come into the new millennium with a culture still rich and with our pride intact. We did this by the sheer will and determination that have always been basic principles of our culture. The Long Walk retaught us the value of these.

Harry Walters

HARRY WALTERS
Director of the Hatathli Museum, Diné College

THE CHEROKEES

By 1836, the Choctaw, Creek, and Chickasaw Nations had been removed west of the Mississippi. Only Seminoles holding out in Florida swamps and the Cherokees remained. In December 1835 a handful of Cherokees, none authorized to speak for their nation, signed the Treaty of New Echota, ceding the last of the tribe's ancestral lands.

The Army began the first forced migrations in 1837, as resistant Cherokees were taken west by barge, rail, and road. In May 1838, the Army forced Cherokees into internment camps, where they were held for months in squalid conditions. Following the disastrous early migrations, the Cherokees were allowed to conduct their

own removal. They chose a northern route. In the fall of 1838, the first of 13 detachments totaling about 12,000 people set out. Conditions in the internment camps, a long winter, scarce provisions, and despair took a terrible toll. In all, 4,000 or more people perished, at least a fourth of the Cherokee Nation.

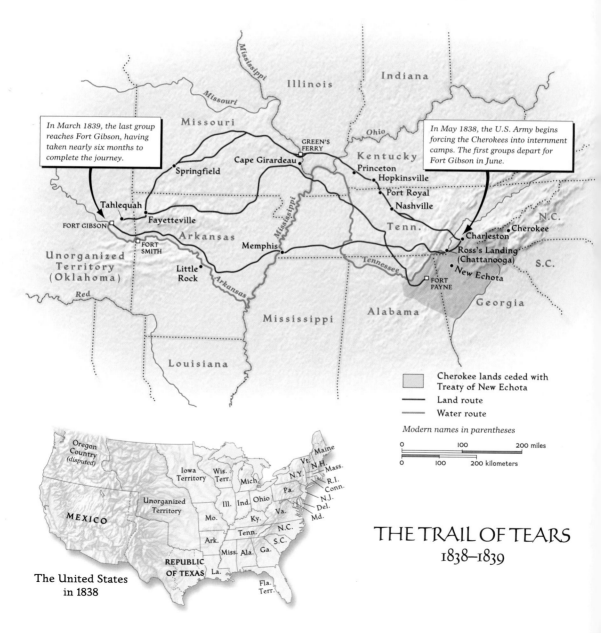

In March 1839, the last group reaches Fort Gibson, having taken nearly six months to complete the journey.

In May 1838, the U.S. Army begins forcing the Cherokees into internment camps. The first groups depart for Fort Gibson in June.

Cherokee lands ceded with Treaty of New Echota
Land route
Water route

Modern names in parentheses

The United States in 1838

THE TRAIL OF TEARS
1838–1839

THE NAVAJOS

By the time the United States assumed control of the Southwest in 1846, the Navajos had been warring with the Spanish and the New Mexicans for over 250 years. Fighting continued with the Americans. In 1862, Gen. James H. Carleton, territorial commander in the Southwest, proposed removing all Navajos from their homeland east to Fort Sumner and a barren reservation called Bosque Redondo. In a campaign led by Kit Carson, more than 8,000 Navajos were herded into Forts Canby and Wingate. From there, the first group of Navajos began its 400-mile journey in August 1863. They were detoured north to be paraded through the streets of Santa Fe, the territorial capital. It took the Navajos three weeks to reach the newly built Fort Sumner, where hundreds would perish from disease, starvation, and exposure. By 1868, the reservation was a national scandal, and too costly to maintain. The Navajos were allowed to return to their ancestral home.

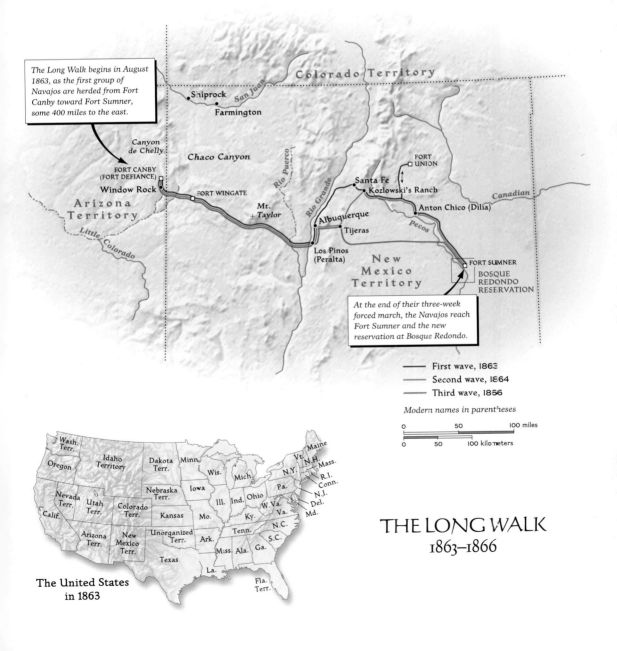

The Long Walk begins in August 1863, as the first group of Navajos are herded from Fort Canby toward Fort Sumner, some 400 miles to the east.

At the end of their three-week forced march, the Navajos reach Fort Sumner and the new reservation at Bosque Redondo.

—— First wave, 1863
—— Second wave, 1864
—— Third wave, 1866

Modern names in parentheses

0   50   100 miles
0   50   100 kilometers

The United States in 1863

THE LONG WALK
1863–1866

IT IS LATE AT NIGHT. YOU AND YOUR FAMILY wake to sounds that fill your hearts with dread: marching feet, voices barking orders in a foreign tongue. The door bursts open. Uniformed men with guns force you into a growing crowd of weeping, frightened people. The night fills with the cries of friends and neighbors and the curses of men who show no pity as they shout orders to march toward an unknown destination. Some people—the weak, the old, the very young—fall and never rise again. Behind you, shots ring out and homes burn in crackles of fire. Terrible as it is, this night is only the beginning, for soon in crowded, disease-ridden camps, the dying will truly begin.

This was a story all too familiar in the 20th century, yet it is neither a story limited to modern times nor one that happened in a distant land. More than a century ago, within the borders of the United States, this is what happened to the Cherokees of the Southeast and the Navajos of the desert Southwest. Between 1838 and 1866, tens of thousands of human beings, guilty of no other crime than being Indian in the face of Manifest Destiny, were rounded up without mercy and driven from their beloved homelands. Each nation was forced to walk what the Cherokees have so eloquently described as a "Trail of Tears."

Why should we concern ourselves today with the histories of the Cherokees and the Navajos? It is not just because their stories of trust and betrayal are as moving and complex as anything in Greek tragedy. There is inspiration to be found here, as well. Hard as their roads of loss and grief were, the Navajos and Cherokees persevered. Today, despite past attempts to destroy their tribal roots, the Navajos and Cherokees have not only maintained their distinct cultural identities as Native American nations, they remain the two largest tribes within the United States, numbering over half a million people. They have not just survived—they have managed to thrive.

Although their stories of survival were woven from different

threads, both native nations found strength by adapting to the new while remaining true in their hearts to the old. Deep spiritual beliefs and inspiration drawn from the sacred land itself brought light to even their darkest hours.

Though deceived and dispossessed, at times divided from within, they endured as unique tribal nations. Though lied to, they kept their words, perhaps most dramatically in the way each nation honored its pledge to never again make war against the United States. Instead, the Navajos and Cherokees have fought for their country. From World War I, when unbreakable codes based on native languages were first employed, to the Persian Gulf, Navajos and Cherokees, as well as other Native American peoples, have been among the first to volunteer to serve in the U.S. military.

As a man of American Indian heritage, I have always been inspired by these stories. My own Abenaki ancestors were among the first native peoples of this continent to survive attempts to wipe us out and drive us from our original homelands. The hard roads walked by the Cherokees and Navajos symbolize the experience of nearly all our indigenous nations. In an even larger sense, these stories epitomize what is best and most enduring about the human spirit.

The Navajos and Cherokees returned from their trails of tears to travel once more along paths of beauty. Walk a way with them now. It is worth the journey.

Overseen by a mounted white soldier, a Cherokee party heads west on the Trail of Tears before the main exodus of the Cherokee Nation in the fall of 1838. In a letter to his wife, Capt. L.B. Webster wrote on June 19, 1838, "It was pitiful to behold the women and children who suffered exceedingly."

JOSEPH BRUCHAC

THE NAVAJOS AND CHEROKEES
ANCIENT ORIGINS

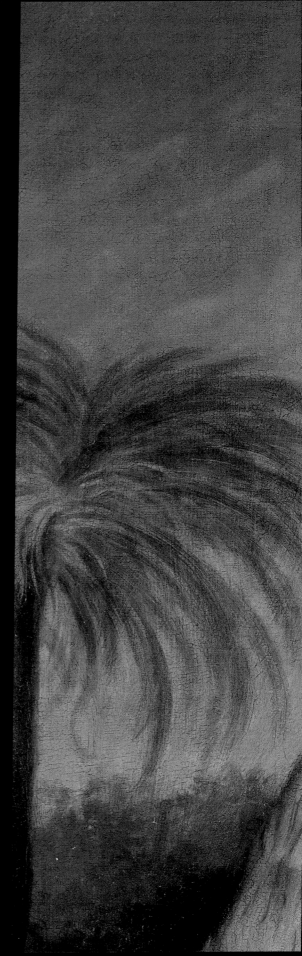

In Tsegehi,

In the house made of dawn,

In the house made of evening twilight,

In the house made of dark cloud,

In the house made of male rain,

In the house made of dark mist,

In the house made of female rain,

In the house made of pollen,

In the house made of corn beetle,

Where the dark mist curtains the doorway...

from The Night Chant
Traditional Navajo, translated in 1897

FORMULA FOR TREATING THE CRIPPLER
(Rheumatism)

Yu! O Red Woman, you have caused it.

You have put the intruder under him.

Ha! now you have come from the Sun Land

You have put the small red seats,

with your feet resting upon them.

Ha! now they have moved swiftly away from you.

Relief is accomplished.

Let it not be for one night alone.

Let the relief come at once.

written by Gahuni,
from The Sacred Formulas of the
Cherokees *(1891)*

IN THE ANCIENT LAND OF THE CHEROKEES,

the leaves have fallen from the trees and the songs of the birds of summer can no longer be heard. The people of the Deer Clan are gathered in their lodge dug into the earth, walled with upright posts, and roofed with bark and straw thatch.

Everyone grows silent as an elder shuffles to the place saved for him close to the fire. His long gray hair, parted in the middle, hangs over his shoulders. He wears a colorful shirt made of patterned trade cloth, and about his neck hangs a shell pendant carved with an ancient design. The old man spreads his hands wide over the fire and begins to speak.

Long ago, all was water here. The animal people lived in Galun'lati, the Sky World above the arch of the sky. But all was not well, it was too crowded. The animals wondered what was below the water. At last Dayuni'si, Water Beetle who is called Beaver's grandchild, volunteered to see.

Water Beetle darted first in one direction over the surface of the water and then in the next, but found no firm place to rest. Then Water Beetle dove down, deeper and deeper until it reached the bottom. There was soft mud there. Water Beetle brought it up to the surface where it began to grow and spread until it became this island we call the Earth. To keep it from sinking

OPPOSITE: In plains-style headdress, medicine man Two Trees Cannon calls on his Cherokee ancestors as he blesses a western-style tipi near Cherokee, North Carolina.

PAGES 12-13: Sunlight outlines Ledge House, an ancient Anasazi dwelling tucked into a sandstone alcove of Canyon de Chelly. The canyon provided a near-perfect hiding place for Navajos evading U.S. Army soldiers.

PRECEDING PAGES: This portrait of Cherokee Chief Cunne Shote was painted by Francis Parsons in 1762. The calm gaze of "Stalking Turkey" seems to hold the certainty that despite their trials, his people would prevail.

back beneath the water, the island was fastened to the sky with a cord at each of its four corners.

Because the new Earth was too soft and wet to walk upon, someone had to dry it and make it ready. Great Buzzard was sent to do this. He flew low over the Earth, drying it with his wings. By the time he reached the country of the Aniyunwiya, he was tired. He flew so low that his wings began to strike the Earth. Each time his wings struck, he made a valley, and when his wings lifted he made a mountain. That is why the country of the Aniyunwiya is full of mountains and valleys to this day.

When the Earth was dried, the animals came down. All was dark, and so the sun was set in the sky to give light. At first the sun was too close to this Earth, burning everything. So it was raised the width of seven hands above the sky, just under the sky arch.

People were made only after the animals and the plants. The first man was Kanati, the Hunter. The first woman was Selu, the Corn Mother. We do not know who made them. But we do know that there is another world beneath this one. It is like ours in every way except that the seasons are different. When it is summer here, it is winter there.

FAR TO THE WEST, IN NAVAJO COUNTRY,

deep within Canyon de Chelly, a multisided house made of logs and covered with earth seems as much a part of the land as the stones around it. It is not far from *Tse'na'ashje'ii*, the solitary pinnacle called Spider Rock. Inside this dwelling, the people of the *Táchii'nii*, the Red Running into Water Clan, huddle together for warmth, ready to listen. A gray-haired woman wearing a red blouse and a long skirt and a squash-blossom necklace of silver and turquoise pokes the fire with a stick. Her eyes sparkle like those of a young girl as she begins her own tale of how things came to be:

At the beginning there was a place called Black World where the Spirit People and the Holy People lived. It was small and much like a floating island in a sea of mist. There were cloud columns of white, blue, yellow, and black over each of the four

Ancient pictographs left by Anasazi artists look out from a sandstone wall of Canyon de Chelly. The stance and attire of the square-shouldered figures convey a sense of awe. To create these mysterious images, the artists ground their pigments from minerals, mixed them with animal fat or vegetable oil, and applied them with brushes made of yucca fiber.

corners of that world. Coyote was there and he visited each of those cloud columns.

First Man was formed in the East, where white cloud and black cloud met. With him was formed the white corn. First Woman was formed in the West where yellow cloud and blue cloud came together. With her was formed the yellow corn, the white shell, and turquoise.

Many kinds of Insect Beings lived in that First World. They began to disagree and fight among themselves. Because of that quarreling, all of those who lived in the First World left that place. They rose up, like clouds, to enter the Blue World through an opening to the East. In the Blue World they found Blue Feathered Beings such as Heron and Blue Jay. They found Wolf, Wildcat, Badger, Fox, and Mountain Lion. Those beings were fighting with each other.

Coyote traveled through that Second World. Everywhere there was suffering and sorrow. So First Man made it possible for all of the Beings to leave. They climbed up into the Yellow World through an opening to the South.

In the Third World there were six sacred mountains. A great river crossed the land from North to South. This was the Female River. Another great river crossed from East to West. This was the Male River. Turquoise Boy and White Shell Girl lived in this world without sun.

One day, Coyote saw something in the water. It was a baby, the child of Tééhóóltsodii, Water Monster. Coyote picked that baby up and hid it under his robe. Then it began to rain. There was a great flood. The people climbed higher and higher into the mountains.

First Man planted a cedar tree, then a pine tree, then a male reed to try to reach the top of the sky. At last he planted a female reed and it grew tall enough to reach the Fourth World. The people crowded onto that reed and climbed up as the flood waters rose. When they reached the top, they saw Coyote hiding something. It was the child of Water Monster. They made Coyote give the baby back and when he did so, the water began to go down.

Then the people entered the Fourth World, the Glittering World, the Rainbow World. There First Man and First Woman formed the Four Sacred Mountains from the soil brought by First Man from the Third World. It is among those Four Sacred Mountains, in this Glittering World, that the people live to this day.

These two creation stories from the *Diné* (those we have come to call the Navajos) and the *Aniyunwiya* (the people known to us now as the Cherokees) speak not only of their own origins but of the beginning of all life upon this Earth. Each tale contains basic beliefs that underlie the philosophy and spiritual traditions of these native nations. The stories approach the Earth from two different directions, one beginning high above while the other emerges from the depths. Both describe a universe in which there is balance and cooperation between living things; humans are neither more important nor more knowing than other beings.

Folklorists describe the Cherokee tale of creation, one in which Earth is brought up by one water creature or another from beneath primeval waters, as having the Earth Diver motif. Very similar stories are found throughout the continent, including among the Iroquoian nations of the Northeast, linguistic cousins of the Cherokees. The Earth Diver story is only one of many connections between the Iroquois and Cherokees. It gives strength to theories that envision the two peoples migrating east—the Iroquois branching north while the Cherokees turned toward the southeast.

The story told by the Diné is an example of another common motif in American Indian creation myths—that of Emergence. Among the Navajos, this traditional story can be told on several levels according to the audience's level of understanding.

Painstakingly pecked into stone, this Navajo petroglyph emanates mystery and power. Found on the walls of a canyon in northwestern New Mexico, it depicts a Yei or Holy Being called Fringed Mouth from the Night Way Ceremony.

The first level, *Ho'zhǫ́ǫ́jí Hane'* or the Beauty Way Story, emphasizes knowledge that is good and wholesome, and is directed to children. The second level is *Diyin Kehjí Hane'*, the Holy People Way, and the third is *Hatáál Kehjí Hane'*, the Ceremonial Way. The fourth level, *Naaye'ejí Hane'*, Protection Way, deals with evil, death, warfare, and witchcraft, and is directed only to mature audiences who have knowledge of ceremonial protocol. Everything in the Navajos' world is related to the creation story.

The themes that the Cherokee and Navajo stories have in common—journeys, finding new worlds to live in—agree with the theories of origin put forward by archaeologists. Long ago, modern theorists and American Indian elders believe, the Cherokees and Navajos traveled great distances to reach the places where they live today. The questions of where they came from and when they arrived have been the object of scholarly speculation for centuries, with answers that seem to change from one generation to the next.

No one knows for certain how or when the native peoples first walked to this wide continent, how they found the canyon lands of the Southwest, or first entered the great mist-shrouded mountains of the Southeast. Did they emerge from a hole in the Earth? Were they shaped from the soil itself by the hands of gods? Or were they bands of hunters, following game animals across the northland, walking ever southward over the course of many generations? Perhaps we can never know for sure. However, both traditional stories and scientific theories can help those of us who came much later envision how it might have been.

Some of the earliest theories of Native American origins linked all American Indians to the Middle East. Serious attempts were made to

establish a connection between the aboriginal peoples of the Americas and the Lost Tribes of Israel, who, according to the theory, found their way across the Atlantic.

Gradually, the Lost Tribes idea was replaced by the more scientific theory of migration from northern Asia by way of Alaska and Canada. It was first thought that this had occurred in a great wave of human migration about 10,000 years ago when the Ice Age made a temporary land bridge between Asia and North America. But current theories, which fall more in line with Native American traditions, postulate a series of such Asian transpolar migrations beginning more than 25,000 years ago.

It's likely that human beings have been going back and forth between the continents for even longer than that. Anyone who has spent time among the native peoples of Alaska knows that the Bering

Dressed in ornate robes of trade cloth, these three Cherokee leaders—Ostenaco, Cunne Shote, and Pouting Pigeon were brought to London in 1762 by Henry Timberlake, a soldier of fortune from Hanover County, Virginia. When their interpreter died, the three Cherokees were left without a voice in a foreign land.

Strait, with the outermost of its archipelago of islands within sight of Siberia, is not that wide a barrier for travel by boat or even by foot across frozen Arctic ice.

Whether American Indian or Asian, African or European, we humans are restless beings. Curiosity about what lies over the next hill has never been limited to European explorers. In the more than 25,000 years that human beings have been in the Americas, there has been time for migrations to take place not just from north to south, but from south to north, west to east, and back again.

By the time of the first recorded encounters between Europeans and Cherokees and Navajos in the 16th century, each of these Native American nations had established deep spiritual ties to the areas they regarded as their ancient and sacred homelands.

IMPORTANT CLUES TO NAVAJO MIGRATION

can be found in the spoken word. The Navajos and their close cousins, the Apaches, belong to the Athapaskan language family. Groups of people speaking those interrelated languages, whose common ancestors are called *Na-Déné,* can be found in Alaska, Canada, and the American Southwest. It is possible that the Na-Déné language is ultimately related to Sino-Tibetan, the speech family to which Japanese and Chinese belong. The four major subfamilies of Na-Déné are Eyak, Tlingit, Haida, and Athapaskan. The first three are found only north of the present-day Canadian border. The Southwestern speakers of Athapaskan are the Apaches and Navajos.

The study of how speech changes over time, called glottochronology, can be used to estimate how many years have passed between present day and the time members of different groups broke away from a common language. Glottochronologists believe that their work clearly establishes a northern origin for the Navajos. They estimate that about 1,000 years ago, Athapaskan-speaking people began to migrate southward. Anthropologist J. Loring Haskell calculates the divergence between Navajos and Canadian Athapaskan tongues such as Beaver and Dogrib took place about 900 years ago, the separation of Navajos from Jicarilla and San Carlos Apaches about 400 years ago, and from Chiricahua Apaches only about 150 years ago.

Anthropologists also use dental evidence to establish a link

OPPOSITE: The Navajos call this place Kin Na' agai, "White House in between." Dating from a period between 1060 and 1275, White House ruin is one of the best preserved sites in Canyon de Chelly. Perhaps a dozen Anasazi families once lived in the 21 rooms of the cliff house and 60 rooms of the lower pueblo.

between Native Americans and northern Asians. In a given population, traits such as the number of roots, the number of cusps on molars, and other features offer clues for anthropologists. Such patterns are a genetic inheritance that remains stable from generation to generation. Christy B. Turner II, a dental anthropologist, points out that a particular group of dental traits is shared by the original inhabitants of the Americas, the Chinese, the Japanese, the Mongols, and the eastern Siberians. He believes that dental anthropology indicates three different waves of migration to the New World: the Paleo-Indians, the ancestors of the Aleuts and Inuits, and the Na-Déné.

If the Navajos' ancient journey did, indeed, take them down from the far north into the Southwest, they would have encountered strange new worlds of flora and fauna. Along the way, the wide, treeless plains of muskeg and permafrost were gradually replaced by tall mountains with slopes blanketed by great evergreens. Caribou herds and salmon-filled rivers gave way to pronghorn antelope and vast herds of buffalo. Beyond the wide, grassy plains lay an arid landscape of mountains and canyons and painted deserts.

Long ago, Native American pottery served many purposes as vessels for water, food, or ceremonial offerings. Weathered by the elements, these shards now hold only dust and wind where they were found in the hills near Thoreau, New Mexico.

OPPOSITE: His face a map of time, Navajo elder Hoshkay Yazhie gazes through the photographer's lens to future generations.

Archaeology provides evidence of such a migration route for the ancestors of the Navajos and Apaches. Athapaskan implements of bone and stone, campsites, kill sites, and pottery have been found from the plains of Canada down through Montana, Wyoming, Utah, and southern Colorado into the Southwest. During migration, life must have centered on hunting the buffalo and gathering wild plants.

The Athapaskans were not the only people traveling across the great plains. At about that same time, the Numa (the Shoshonean-speaking ancestors of the Utes and Comanches), began their own route of migration that led from the Great Basin Plateau of California and Nevada across Utah and Colorado. When the Na-Déné and Numa met, it seems, a long history of rivalry began. In fact, confrontations between the Na-Déné and Shoshone peoples provide one explanation for the disbursement of the migrating Athapaskans into many different language groups. The oral traditions of the Navajos and Apaches

Woven in a bold geometric pattern called Ganado,
this Navajo rug dates from about 1930.

on one side, and the Comanches and Utes on the other, record the ancient conflict between the two groups. To this day, the Utes and Comanches are still regarded as enemies by the Navajos and Apaches.

No one knows exactly when and from which precise direction these Athapaskan ancestors actually reached the new homeland they called *Dinetah* or how they were greeted by those who had been in the Southwest thousands of years before them. The languages and customs of these Aztec-Tanoan Pueblo peoples differed a great deal from those of the northern Athapaskans.

A bat design painted inside a Mimbres pot hints at the richness of imagery and story in the lives of the Mogollon people, neighbors of the Anasazi who lived more than a thousand years ago along what is now the Arizona-New Mexico border.

The earliest of those first inhabitants of the Southwest built the now famous cliff dwellings in such places as Mesa Verde, Chaco Canyon, and Canyon de Chelly—all of which were deserted by the time of the coming of the whites. The cliff dwellers left their homes after a period of severe drought in the 13th century. One of the theories concerning the abandonment of those elaborately constructed apartment houses of stone, adobe brick, and wood—some of them three stories tall with 80 rooms—was that the Navajos drove away or killed the cliff dwellers.

The Navajos called those early people *Anasazi,* an ancient Athapaskan term that has changed in meaning through time. Though some translate the word as "ancient enemies," the Navajos' creation stories make no mention of hostility between these ancient Pueblos and the Diné. "Ancient ancestors" is a more recent Navajo interpretation of the term, indicating both familiarity and family connection, since according to Navajo tradition, these people once intermarried with Navajos. (The nearby Hopi and other Pueblo Indians favor *Hisatsinom,* their own word for "ancestors.") Navajo creation stories tell of meeting the Cliff Swallow people in the Second Blue World. They called them *Anahj' Din'é*—"people who live alongside" or "neighbors." The word *sa'zi* refers to those who are no longer living.

Anthropologists now believe that the exodus from the great houses built into the caves and niches of sheltered canyons was the result of a combination of factors including sustained droughts and overpopulation. The Athapaskan "invasion" probably played little or no part in the departure of the Anasazi.

Some speculated that the Navajos arrived in the late 15th and early 16th centuries, not long before the Spanish. Thus, the Navajos would never have encountered these earlier canyon dwellers at all. According to this theory, it was not until after the Pueblo Rebellion against Spanish rule in 1680 that the Navajos learned agriculture, weaving, and ceremonials from Pueblo people who sought refuge among them.

But there is now clear evidence that the Navajos were well-established in the Southwest at the time of the coming of the Europeans. The so-called Pueblo cultural traits had already been absorbed into the everyday lives of the Navajo. By the 1500s the Navajos were already weaving, and practicing ceremonies that appear to be deeply influenced by the Pueblos. They were also engaging in sophisticated horticulture.

Navajo oral tradition says that they arrived in the Southwest at about the time of the construction of the Great Pueblo in Chaco Canyon—between A.D. 900 and 1100. Archaeology has begun to substantiate this. Using the science of dendrochronology, or tree ring dating, in what is now western Colorado, ruins of forked pole hogans, a house form used only by Navajos, have been dated to A.D. 1000. Another Navajo homesite, south of Gallup, New Mexico, has been dated to 1380.

In his unpublished paper, "A New Perspective on Navajo Prehistory," Navajo cultural historian Harry Walters discusses how oral traditions contain considerable evidence of an extended period of contact with the Anasazi—the Cliff Swallow People of the Second World and, in the Third World, the Lizard People who lived in pit houses. Walters believes the Anasazi and Navajos interacted freely and intermarried, and that today's Navajos are actually a mixture of Pueblos and Athapaskans.

The Navajos did not, however, adopt the urban lifeways of the crowded pueblos. Instead, they remained in small, seminomadic family bands. Although the bands came together at times to make some decisions, Navajo government was never centralized. The family dwelling, not the communal pueblo, served as both home and symbolic center of their spiritual lives.

Navajo society has always been matrilineal and matrilocal. A traditional extended family group consists of an older woman and her husband, along with her married daughters and their husbands in a cluster of dwellings within shouting distance of each other. Land, property, and decision-making rest with the clan. The men and women of that clan in a family settlement are in charge. Even though a man must, of necessity, marry into other clans since it is forbidden to marry someone of his own clan, most of his possessions are kept at his mother's place, which remains his principal home.

The traditional Navajo dwelling, called a hogan, is a rounded earth-covered house with its door facing the sunrise. The earliest style hogan is the four-forked beam or "male hogan," an inverted cone with a covered entryway. The "female hogan" is six-sided with a corbeled log roof. The Navajo word *hooghan* literally translates as "place home."

The Navajo hogan is both home and symbol of the Navajo world, its roof the Sky, its floor the Earth. Dinetah itself is said by the Navajos to be an immense hogan, its four house posts the mountain peaks which surround their sacred land.

Although the Spanish first arrived in Dinetah in 1540, the colonization of that great expanse of territory where the present-day states of Colorado, New Mexico, Arizona, and Utah come together did not begin until 1598 with the expedition of Don Juan de Oñate. The men of New Spain met resistance from both the Pueblos and the Navajos, but they were persistent. The Pueblos were eventually brought under Spanish control. Soon the Spanish were sending a stream of missionaries, soldiers, and settlers into the Southwest.

FOLLOWING PAGES:
In search of winter-hardy medicinal plants, Two Trees Cannon rides across his ancestral homeland in an area just inside the Georgia border. An apprentice follows close behind to learn the Cherokee ways.

The Navajos, though forced to retreat toward the west, were never conquered by the Spaniards. Their animosity against Europeans deepened because of the practice, engaged in by Spanish soldiers, settlers, and missionaries, of enslaving Indians. When the Pueblos revolted in 1680, some Navajos were their allies in driving out the whites. When the Spanish reconquered the New Mexico Pueblos a few years later, many Pueblo refugees were taken in and protected by the Navajos.

Although the Spanish brought conflict, they also brought something else that would change the lives of the Navajos forever in a positive way—domestic animals. With the advent of horses, sheep, and goats after the arrival of the Spanish, the Navajos would expand their culture while still remaining Diné and become some of the most successful herdsmen the world has ever known. Stories and songs about the new creatures, such as this excerpt from "The War-God's Horse Song," would weave them into the fabric of Navajo life.

My horse's body is like an eagle-plumed arrow;
My horse has a tail like a trailing black cloud...
His mane is made of short rainbows.
My horse's ears are made of round corn.
My horse's eyes are made of big stars.
My horse's head is made of mixed waters.
(From the holy waters—he never knows thirst.)
My horse's teeth are made of white shell...

Before me peaceful,
Behind me peaceful,
Under me peaceful,
Over me peaceful,
All around me peaceful—
Peaceful voice when he neighs...

With these new animals as a part of their lives, the Navajo culture that developed over the next two centuries was one that blended the practices of hunting, agriculture, and herding. Were it not for periodic slave raids by the Spanish, and their own retaliatory raids in which they took livestock and captives, the Navajo way of life might have been seen as idyllic. Even through centuries of intermittent war between themselves and the whites, the Navajos strove to follow a path which, like the double rainbows that arced over their lands, was a way of beauty and blessing.

THE ANCIENT ORIGIN OF THE CHEROKEES

is shrouded in mystery. A lack of hard data, however, has not stood in the way of scholarly imagination. In 1823, John Haywood made the first serious study of Cherokee origins. He asserted that they were the descendants of two distinct nations that had migrated from Asia. The Cherokees were, in his estimation, linked to the ancient Hebrews and the Hindus. Haywood and others based such beliefs on the stories told them by Cherokees of their time.

In tales they interpreted as "traditional" legends, events including the expulsion from Eden, the Tower of Babel, and Moses and the crossing of the Red Sea were all related in a Cherokee context. Clear evidence, these scholars concluded, of their amazing claims. James Adair's *History of the American Indians,* published in 1775, also refers to such Cherokee myths as proof of their Hebrew origin.

Contemporary scholars, however, agree that the Biblical stories told by the Cherokees are just that—stories learned from Christian missionaries and then retold in Cherokee. In a similar way, stories from England of Jack the Trickster, who outwits those more powerful than himself, and African traditional tales have been absorbed into Native American cultures up and down the eastern seaboard.

A more serious oral tradition of Cherokee migration was recorded in 1896 by Sakiya Sanders, a member of the traditional Keetoowah Society and an elected member of the Cherokee Senate. Published as "A Cherokee Vision of Eloh," in the bilingual newspaper the *Indian Chieftain* in Vinita, Oklahoma, it also includes Biblical elements such as a house built to reach the heavens and a great flood, treating Cherokee history all the way from the ancient past to the coming of the whites with Biblical imagery. It speaks of seven Cherokee clans traveling from the flooded country to a land "more dry and suitable to their liking" while leaving five lost clans behind them. Some Cherokee scholars have interpreted this as an ancient migration not from the north but from South America, but there is little evidence for this theory.

If the ancient ancestors of the Cherokees came from the north as did those of the Navajos, then it was in one of those waves of migration that took place many thousands of years earlier. The Cherokee language, unlike the Algonkian tongues of their southeastern neighbors, is Iroquoian. It is closely related to the languages spoken by the Haudenaunonee of the northeastern woodlands.

Common traditions and certain aspects of material culture, such as the Iroquois unnotched arrow point, further strengthen the case for such links between Iroquois and Cherokees. One theory is that the ancestors of both peoples first moved from the Appalachian Mountain region north to the Great Lakes. At some time, more than a thousand years ago, some of those Iroquoians split off, moving south through Ohio, Pennsylvania, and Virginia to become the Cherokees.

Archaeological evidence indicates that the Cherokee culture was in place in the Southeast sometime between A.D. 1000 and 1300, about the same time the Navajos reached Dinetah. Sites contain such things as shell gorgets, triangular projectile points, and ceramics which are connected to later Cherokee life. Roy S. Dickens, an anthropologist from Georgia State University, believes that these sites were forerunners of Cherokee town centers.

Like the Navajos encountering the cities of the Anasazi, those early Cherokee immigrants found themselves in the presence of other native peoples who had developed deeply spiritual and ceremonial relationships to the natural world. They entered the region of that widespread culture archaeologists have called Mississippian, a way of life spread over most of the Southeast and the lower Mississippi region

Eastern Cherokee tribal member Gene Crowe and his family visit Kituwah mound near Bryson City, North Carolina, in late autumn. A gathering place considered to be the Cherokees' place of origin, the mound has recently returned to tribal ownership.

In "She Speaks for Her Clan," Cherokee artist Dorothy Sullivan depicts the Seven Cherokee clans, from left to right: Wolf, Wild Potato or Bear, Bird, Blue, Deer, Paint, and Long Hair, also known as Twister or Wind. Membership in Cherokee clans is inherited through the mother.

from Illinois and Indiana south through Louisiana and Georgia and west as far as Missouri and Texas.

The Mississippian tradition, which began around A.D. 900, was based upon the introduction of new cultivated plants that had been developed by the great agricultural societies of Mexico. These varieties of corn, beans, and squash returned high yields with a minimum of cultivation and provided the nutrition needed to support larger populations and sustain sizable urban centers. Since the areas farmed were always river bottoms, where yearly floods deposited fertile silt and discouraged the growth of deeply rooted grasses, the only tools needed for planting were hoes and digging sticks.

The physical and ceremonial layout of Mississippian villages also showed the influence of Mexico, with temple mounds and artifacts much like those farther to the south. The typical Mississippian town, always close to a river, consisted of a central temple mound with the sacred fire burning at its heart. Around it were other smaller mounds, public structures, and the homes of the priests and leaders. A stockade was sometimes built to surround the temple complex. One of the greatest of these ancient cities, Cahokia (in present-day Illinois), was founded around A.D. 600. It survived for more than 700 years and had over 10,000 inhabitants in 1200, making it the largest city north of Mexico on the North American continent.

Like the Anasazi, the Mississippian city dwellers apparently experienced certain problems common to cities. For one, their urban centers were a breeding ground for diseases. Fortunately, pre-Columbian America was free of the great range of diseases that the domestication of animals had brought to Europeans. (Infectious diseases such as smallpox, which came from cowpox among cattle, bubonic plague, influenza, and measles were either spread by or originated from animals.) Although these epidemic diseases were not present, physical anthropologists have found evidence of tuberculosis and endemic intestinal parasites among the Mississippians. It appears that by 1450 a large area in the heartland of Middle Mississippi became depopulated, probably due in part to disease and the depletion of natural resources.

From the mid-15th century on, the major centers of Mississippian population appear to have been abandoned. Even so, Mississippian ways had already deeply influenced other cultures in the region, such

as the Cherokees. Smaller Mississippian cities continued to thrive until the coming of Europeans. When the Spanish explorer Hernando de Soto visited several Mississippian centers in 1540, he left behind an epidemic of smallpox. It was the first of a great drowning wave of European plagues that would wipe out as much as 90 percent of the population of the Southeast and bring an end at last to the city cultures of the Mississippi.

The Cherokees, like the Navajos, had been a culture focused upon hunting and gathering for subsistence before they reached their eventual homeland. And like the Navajos, the Cherokees showed themselves able to adapt to a new way of life. Deer remained the primary source of food and meat for the people, while the Three Sisters agriculture of corn, beans, and squash that sustained the Mississippians was wholeheartedly accepted. One of the most important Cherokee traditional stories is that of Kanati, the Hunter, and Selu, the Corn Mother. From that first man and woman and their twin boys spring the Cherokee traditions of male hunting and female agriculture. In that powerful tale, corn comes from the body of Selu herself, growing out of the Earth after she is buried.

The Green Corn Ceremony was the most important event of the year for Mississippian peoples, and it held central importance for the Cherokees as well. A festival of renewal and thanksgiving, it took place in midsummer when the first ears of corn were ripe. At that annual Busk or First Fruits Ceremony, the sacred fire was ritually rekindled, the laws of the nation were recited, ceremonial songs and dances were performed, and the sins of the past year (short of murder) were forgiven. There is little in modern life to compare it with. Anthropologist Charles Hudson suggests that we would only have something approaching the Green Corn Ceremony if Thanksgiving, New Year's festivities, Yom Kippur, Lent, and Mardi Gras were combined in one event.

Many symbols in traditional Cherokee art are the same as those found in the ruins of ancient Mississippian towns. The importance of the number seven among the Cherokees may also have come from the cultures of the Southeast: There are seven Cherokee clans, seven directions, and seven holy woods. The fire burning at the center of the sacred mound has the same ceremonial importance among the

OPPOSITE: Cane Creek Falls near Spencer, Tennessee, was only one of the beloved places left behind by the grieving Cherokees. The Trail of Tears passed near this place, now part of Fall Creek Falls State Park, the largest state park in Tennessee. Its 19,000 acres, half set aside for wilderness, preserves some of the landscape just as those who were on the trail might have seen it.

A southern Cherokee man named Climbing Bear faces the camera in 1888 dressed in the stiff and formal clothing of the period.

PRECEDING PAGES: Now extinct Carolina parakeets fly through a Cherokee village during harvest time in this rendering of Native American life before European contact.

FOLLOWING PAGES: This ridgetop view south of Spencer, Tennessee, looks west. The Trail of Tears passed through the forest in the distance.

Cherokees as it did among the old city dwellers of the Southeast. To this day, the Cherokees tell of how, until the Trail of Tears, the fire always burned at the mound at Kituwah, the mother settlement near present-day Bryson City, North Carolina.

At the center of each Cherokee village was a plaza with a council house, a large circular building on an earthen mound, where village council meetings were held. Decisions were reached by democratic consensus; the women were as free to be heard as the men. Like the Iroquois, the Cherokees placed women at the center of their culture.

By the time the Europeans encountered them, the Cherokees were the most influential and widespread of all the Indian nations in their region. When de Soto made his way through the Cherokee homelands in 1540, he encountered native towns with populations of hundreds or even thousands of Cherokees. They dominated an area including the western part of present-day North Carolina, South Carolina, West Virginia and Virginia, most of Tennessee, Kentucky, northern Georgia, and Alabama. Not until 1760 would the Cherokee people suffer their first real military losses—to the English—and be forced by treaty to cede part of their territory.

ALTHOUGH BOTH THE CHEROKEES AND

the Navajos have often been characterized as warriors, or even "bloodthirsty raiders," it is important to recognize the place that war held among both cultures before the coming of Europeans. In both nations, the idea of all-out war, of fighting for territory or seeking the total defeat of an enemy nation, was a foreign concept.

Among the Navajos, fighting an enemy might be necessary, but it resulted in a spiritual pollution which could only be cleansed through ceremony. Raiding on a small scale took place, but more often than not the relations between Pueblo neighbors and the Navajos in the pre-European period appear to have been characterized by respect and mutually beneficial trade. Retaliatory war against the Spanish and the New Mexicans became necessary for survival.

Similarly, for the Cherokees, war was not war as Europeans knew it. Fighting usually took the form of raids by small groups of warriors upon their enemies. The aim was to restore balance, for if a Cherokee was killed by an enemy, his spirit could not go to the Darkening Land until his death had been avenged.

Among both Navajos and Cherokees, if captives were taken in a raid they might be tortured or killed or, just as likely, adopted into the tribe. For the Cherokees, it was the War Women—brave, respected women who accompanied war parties—who decided the fate of such captives. Both Navajos and Cherokees adopted white captives into their nations. Many of those white men and women, Spanish or English, fully accepted native life, refusing to return to white culture when the opportunity presented itself.

What was it like among the Navajos and the Cherokees in the time before they were forced from their homelands by Europeans? Their daily lives, it seems, were characterized by a deep commitment to maintain spiritual and physical equilibrium and to live in a right relationship among the people and with the land.

The Navajos and Cherokees chose to walk paths of beauty and balance—even as their worlds changed with the coming of European invaders who seemed, at times, unable to recognize the humanity of the native nations they sought to dominate.

In this photograph taken in the 1890s, a Cherokee woman pounds corn by her cabin in the mountains of North Carolina. Such cabins had been in common use by the Cherokees since the mid-1700s. Scenes such as this would have been interrupted by soldiers as they rounded up Cherokees for removal in 1838.

THE NAVAJOS
TO WALK IN BEAUTY

Neya, behind her, from there, ye, Corn Beetle
            Girl, 'eye,
      She comes upon me with blessing, wo,
Before her, from there, ye, Bik'eh hozhoo,
      She comes upon me with blessing, wo,
Behind her, from there, ye, Sa'ah naaghei,
      She comes upon me with blessing, wo,
Behind her, it is blessed,
Before her, it is blessed,
Beneath her it is blessed,
Above her, it is blessed,
All around her it is blessed,
Everywhere, it is blessed, neye 'eya lana heya eye...

    Frank Mitchell (Navajo)

i sing to myself and
think of my father
      teaching me, leaning toward me
      listening as i learned
      "just like this" he would say
      and he would sing those old songs
            into the fiber of my hair,
            into the pores of my skin
            into the dream of my children
      and i am singing now
      for the night
            the almost empty moon
            and the land swimming beneath cold
                  bright stars

    Luci Tapahonso (Navajo)

DINÉ BIKÉYAH—NAVAJO COUNTRY—CONTAINS

some of the most dramatic landscapes in North America. There are deep, blood red canyons, great dark lava flows, huge rock shapes so sculpted by wind and water that the human imagination can easily accept them as ancient beings transformed into stone. Above the painted deserts and grassy upland plains, mountain slopes green with aspen, pine, and cedar rise to snow capped peaks. Rich alluvial valleys spread out like opened hands, gray-green with sagebrush and darkened by groves of piñon and gnarled juniper.

As awe-inspiring as the land may be, the heavens, of course, have their own epic scope. Earth and sky hold each other in balance. The wide, incredibly open skies are brilliant with uncountable stars at night. The land below is painfully dry much of the year. Whirlwinds ripple through the tall, dry grasses and dance across the dusty soil. In the brief seasons of rain, Diné Bikéyah is the land of male rain, the heavy downpour, and female rain, the rain that falls lightly to caress the earth. The immense sky arch is the site of pyrotechnic displays of lightning accompanied by the deep drum of thunder.

When the brief seasons of moisture arrive, the land glows with the brilliant hues of innumerable wildflowers. Clouds of many shapes and colors dance in the sky or spread dark nimbus wings from horizon to horizon like giant birds. Nowhere on Earth are rainbows more beautiful. The Navajos incorporate them into religious traditions; they

OPPOSITE: Lillie Joe Hathaley looks to the east from the doorway of a hogan, the traditional Navajo dwelling that is both house and symbolic model of the universe.

PAGES 50-51: Sunrise illuminates a red butte east of Gallup, New Mexico. Such landforms inspired the shape of the traditional Navajo hogan.

PRECEDING PAGES: Eugene B. Joe and his aunt, Lillie Joe Hathaley, complete a sandpainting as Eugene's father, James, watches in silent approval.

see them as paths of beauty and the visible bodies of Holy People.

The Navajos look not only to the great Father Sky, but also to four sacred mountains: East Mountain, *Sisnaajiní* (Mt. Blanca in Colorado); South Mountain, *Tsoodził* (Mt. Taylor in New Mexico); West Mountain, *Dook'o'oosłííd* (San Francisco Peaks in Arizona); and North Mountain, *Dibe' Nitsaa* (Hesperus Peak in Colorado). These highly visible peaks mark the traditional boundaries of the Navajos' heartland and form the mythic posts of the great hogan encompassing Dinetah.

In the decades following the American Civil War, a man named Washington Matthews entered that great hogan when he traveled to the newly defined Navajo Reservation. At that time it was believed that the cultures of the Navajos and all other Native Americans were about to vanish. Unless their "primitive" traditions could be recorded by Matthews and other ethnologists, they would be lost forever. Matthews, however, was struck by both the enduring ways of the Navajos and the powerful poetry in the songs and stories he heard.

Among the stories Matthews wrote down was the tale of how the four sacred mountains were created. In the decades that followed, other versions of such stories, crucial to all Navajo healing ceremonies, were collected by other non-Navajos. Variations are found from one recorded telling to the next, in part because these stories are so sacred that it has been the Navajo custom never to tell the story fully to an outsider, or at least to change certain crucial details in the telling. Thus, the following version of how the Navajos say their sacred mountains came to be is drawn from a number of sources.

It was the time just after the Emergence. Áłtsé Hastiin, First Man, and Áłtsé Asdzáán, First Woman, got together with Bits'íís Dootł'izh, Blue Body, who is also known as Water Sprinkler, and Bits'íís tizhin, Black Body, who is also known as Haashch'éé zhiní, the God of Fire. It was time, they decided, to build sacred mountains like those that had existed in the previous world. Those mountains would be needed so the people to come could properly do the ceremonies that the Holy People would give them.

First Man asked how those mountains should be placed.

"We shall place them as they were in the world below," First Woman answered.

Then she threw a white shell taken from the eastern mountain in the previous world. Where it landed, to the east, they placed Sisnaajiní. They fastened it to the Earth with a bolt of lightning and decorated it with white shells, white lightning, white corn, dark cloud, and male rain. Rock Crystal Boy and Rock Crystal Girl were placed here to dwell.

Next First Woman threw a turquoise stone. Where it landed, to the south, they placed Tsoodził. They fastened it to the Earth with a great stone knife, thrust through from top to bottom. Tsoodził was adorned with turquoise, with dark mist, with female rain, and with different kinds of game animals. The Boy Who Carries One Turquoise and The Girl Who Carries One Grain of Corn were placed in this mountain to dwell.

First Woman threw yet another sacred stone, a piece of abalone shell. It landed to the west and there they placed Dook'o'oosłííd. It was fastened to the Earth with a sunbeam. Then it was adorned with abalone shell, with black clouds, male rain, yellow corn, and all sorts of wild animals. A yellow cloud was spread over Dook'o'oosłííd, and White Corn Boy and Yellow Corn Girl were placed to dwell there.

Now First Woman threw a piece of jet to the north. Where it landed, not far from the place of emergence, Dibe' Nitsaa was placed. They fastened it to the Earth with a rainbow and adorned it with black beads, dark mist, many kinds of plants, and many wild animals. Over it they spread a covering of darkness and they placed Pollen Boy and Corn Beetle Girl within this mountain to dwell.

And so it was that the four sacred mountains were created and the sacred boundaries of Dinetah were set upon the land.

WITHIN THESE BOUNDARIES, IN THAT GREAT hogan, the Navajos were meant to live. As long as they could remain in Dinetah, among those beloved sacred mountains, their lives would be blessed. They would live in balance and beauty and walk in the way of *ho'zho*, a Navajo word that has been translated many ways. Some have said it means harmony, others that it means natural balance or beauty, health, good fortune, or even happiness. In fact, it means all these things and more.

In the world view of the Diné, when things are in balance, there is harmony; beauty and happiness will naturally follow. It is the job of the *Hataałii*, the Navajo singer and medicine man, to help restore that balance through the ancient ceremonials, the Blessingways. The songs and stories within those Ways, centered around *Diné Bahane'*, the Navajo Creation Story, are meant to generate an atmosphere of ho'zho.

As Frank Mitchell explained in his autobiography, *Navajo Blessingway Singer*, "There is a set phrase *Sa'ah Naaghái Bik'eh Hózhóón* to be used at the end of each song, by which it is made more holy and more lasting so that anything that is accomplished will have no end. [It means] according to this, everything is blessed." This constantly repeated phrase might also be translated as "I am, according to the renewal of life, blessing everywhere."

Blessing everywhere, the renewal of life, beauty and balance, happiness and harmony—these concepts are deeply embedded in every aspect of everyday Navajo life. The Navajos say these things are evident in the world around them—where things naturally exist in pairs that balance each other: Earth and Sky, Female and Male, Dry and Moist, Moon and Sun, North and South, East and West. While the universe is an orderly system, it also includes good and evil, safety and danger, life and death.

Navajo weavers display their rugs in a photograph taken in Bluff, Utah, around 1902. Once sold for only a few dollars each, they are now worth tens of thousands of dollars.

In Canyon de Chelly, Navajo weaver Sally Sam passes on the craft said to have been given to the Navajos long ago by Spider Woman. Perhaps it was in this very canyon, where the Anasazi once lived, that weaving became part of Navajo life. Cotton woven into cloth a thousand years ago has been unearthed in the ruins of Antelope House.

There came a time when an important decision had to be made. Would Death come into the world? First Man and First Woman talked about it as they stood by the water. Then each of them picked up a dry stick.

"If this stick sinks when it is thrown into the water, then Death will come into the world," each of them said.

The sticks floated. But then Coyote, who was also there, picked up a pebble. "If this floats," he said, "Death will not come into the world."

The pebble, of course, sank. First Man and First Woman were not happy, but then they realized that Coyote was right. Without Death, there would be so many people that they would fill up the world. It was right for people to die and for their bodies to return to the Earth.

When the first person did die, a woman who lay there upon the Earth without breath in the bright sunlight, the people decided that it had to be the Sun who had killed her because it was the Sun who gave life to everything.

"That is true," said the Sun. "Just as I have given, so it must be given back to me. That way there will always be balance in the world."

And so it is to this day.

This concept of a naturally balanced universe is widespread throughout native North America, as is the belief that the loss of balance may lead to physical and spiritual sickness. Healing ceremonies, however, can diagnose the source of such illness and restore the right

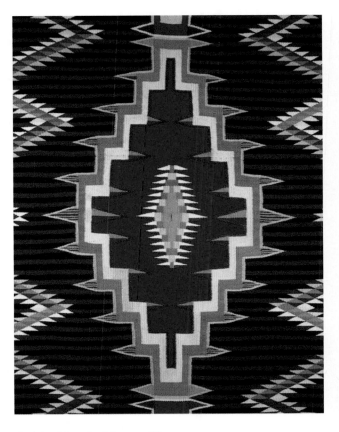

Its vivid hues and patterns recalling the hills and mountains of the Southwest, a Navajo rug echoes a weaver's vision of her world. Over the years, Navajo weavers have developed their own distinctive regional styles.

relationship. No native nations have developed a body of ceremonial practices more complex or lyrically powerful than the Navajo Healing Ways, which came into being at the very beginning of life in this Fourth World.

Soon after the Holy People emerged into this Glittering World, the first Blessingway took place. Navajos regard *Hózhǫǫjí,* the Blessingway Ceremony, as the centralmost of their religious traditions. Not only is it generally acknowledged as the first ceremony to originate from the Holy People, but all other ceremonials are organized by Blessingway and have segments of Blessingway within them.

According to Mike Mitchell, a Navajo elder and traditional historian, there are four main versions of the Blessingway, each corresponding to a period in Navajo history. The first is the Original Blessingway, which relates the story of Changing Woman, her discovery as a baby by First Man, her coming of age, the birth of the Hero Twins, and their journey to their father, the Sun. Here

Ohwo-wo-Songwi, a Corn Dancer from San Ildefonso Pueblo, posed for the camera of Edward S. Curtis. The Pueblo cultures of the Southwest have been a strong influence on the Navajos, who have attended Pueblo feast days, corn dances, and other ceremonies in great numbers through the years.

is the start of that epic tale:

There were many problems in the Fourth World. Evil monsters appeared and began to kill the people. One day, the Holy People saw a cloud form over Ch'óol'į'í. Talking God, one of the Holy People, went there to see what he could find. On the eastern slope, he found a baby girl. She was wrapped in mist, clouds, and rainbow. This baby girl was Asdzáá Náádleełí, Changing Woman. Talking God took her to the house of First Man and First Woman, who raised her.

Within twelve days Changing Woman grew to womanhood. On that twelfth day, all of the Holy People came together to perform a ceremony for the womanhood of First Man and First Woman's foster daughter. Thus it was that the first kinaaldá, the woman's puberty ceremony, took place. From the songs and prayers of that ceremony came the Blessingway. So it was from the very start of her life that Changing Woman brought goodness to the people. But there were still many evil monsters.

Now Changing Woman went to live in her own hogan at the Mountain Around Which Traveling is Done. For a long time she walked about that mountain. Then, one day, the spirit of the Sun came to her and she became pregnant. She gave birth to the Hero Twins. Their names are Naayéé Neez ghánii, Monster Slayer and To'ba'jísh chíní, Born For Water.

Like their mother, the Hero Twins grew to adulthood in only twelve days. Seeing how the monsters were killing people, they determined that these creatures needed to be destroyed. They went to see their father, the Sun, who tested them in various ways to be sure they were indeed his children. After passing his tests, Monster Slayer was given a bow with arrows of lightning that he successfully used to destroy the monsters.

The destruction of those monsters and the sickness that then came over Monster Slayer mark the end of the original Blessingway, but not the end of the story. Protection Way Blessingway is the ceremony for Monster Slayer, the hero twin who killed the monsters but became ill as a result. This ceremony demonstrates how sacred all life is to the Navajos, for even the destruction of terrible monsters brings sickness to the one who destroys them.

In a similar way, a Navajo who killed an enemy was also spiritually compromised. In fact, the very act of going to war, whether the enemy is encountered or not, shifts a person away from the norms of ho'zho. Contamination that comes from destructive forces can bring illness. The Protection Way Blessingway offers a means to restore balance and health to a person who has struck or killed an enemy. Evil Way and Enemy Way are purification ceremonies contained within that second Blessingway.

The third of the Blessingways is Bringing Back Song from the West. This Way deals with how Changing Woman brought the matrilineal clan system to the Navajo people. This event probably occurred after the Navajos arrived in Dinetah, gave up the wandering life of hunting, and settled into being pastoral agriculturists. In addition to being a ceremony of healing, Bringing Back Song also marks an important stage in the development and solidification of Navajo culture.

The last of the Blessingways is Field Song Blessingway, almost certainly the most recent, for it is the only one which makes any mention of the domestic livestock that became part of Navajo life after the coming of the Spanish. Conversely, it could be said that the lack of any reference to the horses and sheep that became so deeply valued by the Navajos in their other ceremonials indicates that the three earlier Blessingways were in place before the coming of the Europeans in the 16th century.

Field Song Blessingway tells of the renewal of Earth and completes the integration of a Navajo worldview into the spiritual lives of the people. As Harry Walters puts it, "Everything that was not yet organized was then set in place. All the ceremonials were refined and given finishing touches." To this day, the Blessingways remain at the center of Navajo life. They are the ancient heartbeats that keep the traditions of the people alive and carry their culture into the future.

FOLLOWING PAGES: A road across the sky said to be the sacred path traveled by Spider Woman, a rainbow arcs over a butte near the town of Mesita, Arizona, in late afternoon. Rainbow images turn up often in Navajo legends and in their art. Because rainbows are held sacred, a person is never supposed to point at one with a finger. The Navajos see their homeland as the beautiful land of the rainbow, a beloved place their ancestors prayed they would return to as the Long Walk passed by this very place in 1864.

AT THE TIME OF EMERGENCE, AFTER PURIFYING themselves in a sweat lodge, the Holy People met in the first hogan. Designed by Talking God, this house was made of powerful and sacred things. Its doorway opened to the East. Pale dawn, blue sky, evening twilight, and folding darkness were placed to cover that entryway. White shell and turquoise, corn and pollen and waters flowing together, fabrics of yellow cloud and rainbow were all part of that wonderfully imagined archetypal structure.

As it was for the first Blessingway done by the Holy People, later Blessingways of human beings would always take place within the hogan. In fact, only there can things properly come together. More than just a dwelling place, the hogan has always been a source of life, a blueprint of the harmony that must be maintained. Even more modern buildings many Navajos live in today are almost always placed so that the entry door opens to the east, where each new day begins.

To this day, no Navajo home is complete until the proper ceremonies have taken place, including "house songs." The hogans envisioned in these house songs can only be described as magical mansions of the gods, yet such enchantment is not restricted to the homes of the Holy People. As the house songs envision Changing Woman, Talking God, and Calling God with their building materials of white shell and turquoise, dawn, clouds, and corn pollen, some of that same magic and power enters the earthly hogans, making them vibrant with awareness and life.

'ai nai yaya,
> The places in times past, I knew all about them,
> The places in times past, I knew all about them,
> The places in times past, I knew all about them, holaghai,

Neye, Earth Woman, yeye,
> Where she would be, deye, I knew all about it, 'eye

All living plants, 'iye
> Where they would be, deye, I knew all about it, 'eye

All kinds of fabrics, ye,
> Where they would be, deye, I knew all about it, 'eye

Now, Long-Life-Returning, now, Causing-Happiness-
> Everywhere, ne,

Where they would be, deye, *I knew all about it,* 'eye
The places in times past, I knew all about them, holaghai

The language of the house songs awakens us to a world that is marvelously alive. Beams are not merely logs, but Wood Woman. Earth Woman and Mountain Woman provide the building materials. Water Woman and Corn Woman give sustenance for those who live within the hogan's circle of walls.

For the Navajos, the hogan is not just a place to live, it is also their source of health and happiness. As Frank Mitchell put it, "You can't just go and plan things for your future; you have to build a hogan first." Every Navajo hogan is potentially a healing environment. It is the place of Long-Life-Returning and Causing-Happiness-Everywhere.

At the Emergence, First Man and First Woman created a radiantly beautiful young couple from the four directions and the elements of nature. Their names were *Sa'ah Naagháí,* Long Life Boy, and *Bik éh Hózhóón,* Happiness Girl. Although they appeared to vanish physically from the world soon after their creation, their spirits remained. Throughout the Blessingway songs, they are mentioned, as David and Susan McAllester explain in their book *Hogans, Navajo Houses & House Songs,* "as a benediction and invocation."

Long Life Boy and Happiness Girl gave birth to Changing Woman. She arrived in the world when everything was ready for her—the four sacred mountains were in place and the chaos of the former worlds had been replaced by balance and beauty. Changing Woman's arrival also brought into being the *kinaaldá,* held for her when she reached puberty. To this day, young girls take part in the ceremony, a happy and much anticipated occasion. During the four-day-long event, a young woman symbolically becomes Changing Woman as she is both blessed and instructed in what is expected of her as an adult.

IN THE TIME BEFORE THE NAVAJO PEOPLE CAME to Dinetah, they did not have hogans. Their nomadic shelters were probably shaped in a similar rounded form, but they lacked the sturdiness and the spiritual permanence of the hogan.

The first Navajo hogan, like the one made by the Holy People, was called *Ałch'į' Adeez'a'hi,* the forked-stick hogan. According to

Navajo tradition, its shape was that of *Ch'óol'į́'í,* Gobernador Knob, where Changing Woman was found as a baby. This type of hogan, a rather small structure and less common today, is called a Male Hogan. It protects those who live within.

Every aspect of building a male hogan is marked by reverence and symbolic activity. The site is carefully selected, far from burial places and not too close to water. The main post beams, usually cut from cedar or pine, are forked at the top and are cut only after asking permission from the Holy People.

Post holes are dug at the south, the west, and the north corners. Offerings, such as the sacred stones associated with each of the directions—white shell for the east, turquoise for the south, abalone for the west and black jet for the north—may be buried in those holes.

The three forked logs are then placed in the post holes and interlocked at the top. The entryway poles, which are referred to as the "fourth pole," are propped against that framework from the direction of the sunrise and spaced to make an eastern doorway. The sides are then filled in with brush and juniper poles, and the whole structure is covered with earth. Each step is done mindfully and accompanied by song or prayer.

When the hogan is complete, it is blessed from within by the family head or a Hataałii, who moves about the hogan in the path of the sun, from east to south, west to north, sprinkling cornmeal or pollen on the main posts.

The second type of hogan, the sort most familiar to non-Navajo, is called *Dah dii tł'inii,* the stacked-log hogan. Its shape is that of the mesa near which Changing Woman made her home, the Mountain-Around-Which-Traveling-Was-Done. The round-roofed hogan is a Female Hogan; it cares for its inhabitants as does a mother.

Although the method of constructing a female hogan is different, the same round of ceremonies—from the cutting of the Trees to the blessing of the support posts—takes place. In the stacked-log hogan, logs are laid out horizontally in the shape of a six- or eight-sided log cabin. At some point, five or six feet above the ground, the cribbed logs become shorter and shorter as their ends overlap, forming an interlocked roof dome.

As with the male hogan, the entire structure is chinked to keep out wind and weather, but usually only the roof is covered with earth to make it proof against sparks from the smoke hole. Depending upon the kind of building materials available, these hogans can be large enough to comfortably hold an extended Navajo family of a dozen or more people and their possessions.

Because of its design, a hogan is usually 30 or 40 degrees cooler inside than out during the hot summer months. In the winter it is surprisingly easy to heat, whether from a central hearth or a woodstove. In the center of the roof of every hogan is an opening called a smoke hole, from which a stovepipe usually emerges. The precipitation that comes in through that hole in the roof is not resented by the Navajos. It simply reminds them, as does the soil beneath their feet, that within the hogan they are in balance between Earth and Sky.

A Navajo silversmith displays a concha belt and other examples of his craft. Introduced to the Navajos by the Spanish in the mid-19th century, silversmithing eventually became a means of artistic expression and a way to make a living. Silver and turquoise jewelry could also serve as a mobile bank account to be pawned for needed cash.

Other types of hogans exist, some with four sides, some made of stone, but all follow the same basic single-room pattern and fill the same role as the visible and symbolic center of the material and spiritual worlds. Everyone in the extended family lives inside the hogan or in smaller structures built close by. During the summer months, brush shelters are used.

UNTIL RECENTLY, NAVAJO COMMUNITIES were small, made up of no more than a few extended families centered around a group of hogans. Their use of the arid land as sheep herders, hunters, and farmers, and the fluctuations in weather and the supply of water, required them to move seasonally. Thus one set of hogans might be used in the summer and another in the winter.

Although traditionally they have not lived in towns or cities, the

Under a burnished south-western sky, Navajo riders cross a landscape viewed by their people as owned by no one, but meant to be cared for and shared by all.

Navajos have never been antisocial. Quite the contrary. Their presence in large numbers at healing ceremonies and the large number of Navajos who have been coming for hundreds of years to the feast-days and ceremonials of their Pueblo neighbors is evidence of how much Navajo people rely upon each other for assistance and enjoy good company.

Further, Navajo patterns of ownership indicate a different understanding of property than that of the majority culture, and a sense of unity with other Navajos and the natural world. Personal possessions and livestock, for example, are always privately owned. Farmlands or rangelands, however, are said to "belong" to the family that has traditionally used those lands. Ownership is passed down matrilineally. Thus a man might inherit land from his mother or sisters, but never from his wife's family.

The inheritance of clan is even more important than the inheritance of property. Every Navajo is "born to" the clan of his or her mother. Each Navajo is also "born for" the clan of his or her father. Whenever Navajo people meet each other for the first time, one of the first things they do is to introduce themselves by saying what clans they were born to and born for.

Clan membership establishes the larger circle of one's relatives. Belonging to the same clan, even if there is no blood relation, immediately establishes a strong relationship. Men and women who share the same clan may not marry. This taboo against same-clan unions is so strong that even dancing with a person of the opposite sex who shares your clan is regarded as incestuous behavior.

While one may own material goods and inherit the control and use of farmlands and rangelands, ownership within the larger natural world is quite another story. Aside from water holes and stands of trees close to a family's hogan, water resources and timber areas are seen as communal. Like the sacred mountains, they belong to everyone. Because the Earth is symbolically viewed as a Mother, one may expect to be cared for by the land, but one may not own it or dispose of it in the way one owns, buys, and sells goods. Many of the problems experienced by the Navajos in their dealings with Europeans stem from their very different views of land ownership.

Even Navajos who live in a modern home often have a hogan in their backyard. One of the most popular house plans from the Navajo tribal housing authority, which helps the Navajos build their own homes, is a one-room house of the same shape as a cribbed-roof hogan. The ground plan of Diné College campus in Tsaile, Arizona, is based on the interior of a hogan, and most of the campus buildings are hogan shaped. Harry Walters, the director of the Hatathli Museum at the college, grew up in a traditional six-sided log hogan.

In Scott Thybony's *The Hogan: The Traditional Navajo Home*, Walters describes the hogan as "a miniature universe. It is a replica of the outer universe, and it has the same power."

What is found within a hogan? When entering from the eastern door, one continues to move in a sunwise direction, from left to right about the hearth. The warmth of that hearth, whether it is an open fire surrounded by stones or a potbellied stove, is the life-giving heart of the one-room building. Above the doorway you may see a worn-out wooden fire poker, a protective talisman kept long after it has burned down too far for its original use.

Within the Navajo universe, directions are determined by standing in the west and facing east. This is because the east, or dawn, always offers the purest and holiest form of knowledge. Everything that falls to the right is female. All that falls to the left is male. Thus the northern side of every hogan is female, while the southern side is male. The male and female sides are not exclusively male or female, however, just as every woman and man is a mixture of both male and female. The left side of every woman is described as her male side, while the right side of every man is female.

The western point is the seat of honor and the place for the head of the family or the Hataałii during a ceremony. When the hogan is used in a ceremonial setting, to deal with illness or evil, the male side of the female is emphasized. Thus, during a healing Way, the men sit on the right, or female, side of the hogan, while the women sit on the left side.

Although the original hogans probably contained almost no furnishings aside from a grinding stone, a few tools, and bedding, by the early 19th century the hogan had become a place in which a great many material possessions were efficiently stored. Today cooking utensils are kept near the central fire and foodstuffs are stored in boxes fixed upon the walls. Other things, wrapped in bundles, are stored in the rafters. Bedding and personal items are hidden in trunks against the walls. A loom for rug weaving is set up against the southern wall. There the craftswoman sits and waits until her mind is in balance before she begins to weave. If her thoughts are good and she is in harmony, the design she weaves will be beautiful.

Against the southern side of the hogan is a man's saddle and riding gear, the tools of a skilled herder. There are only a few bulky items of furniture—two beds, several chairs, a table and a dresser—within this hogan. Many things can be stowed away so that most of the floor space will be open. In the open space, the healing Ways can take place.

Once built, a hogan is not moved. Every part of life takes place here—except for death. Navajos believe that when a person dies, the spirit part of them leaves, leaving behind the human remains that can become a potentially destructive element when tampered with. Any place where death has occurred, a battle has been fought, or evil has taken place is not a good place. Negative power remains there, and so it is wise to avoid such a spot. The power that exists in such places

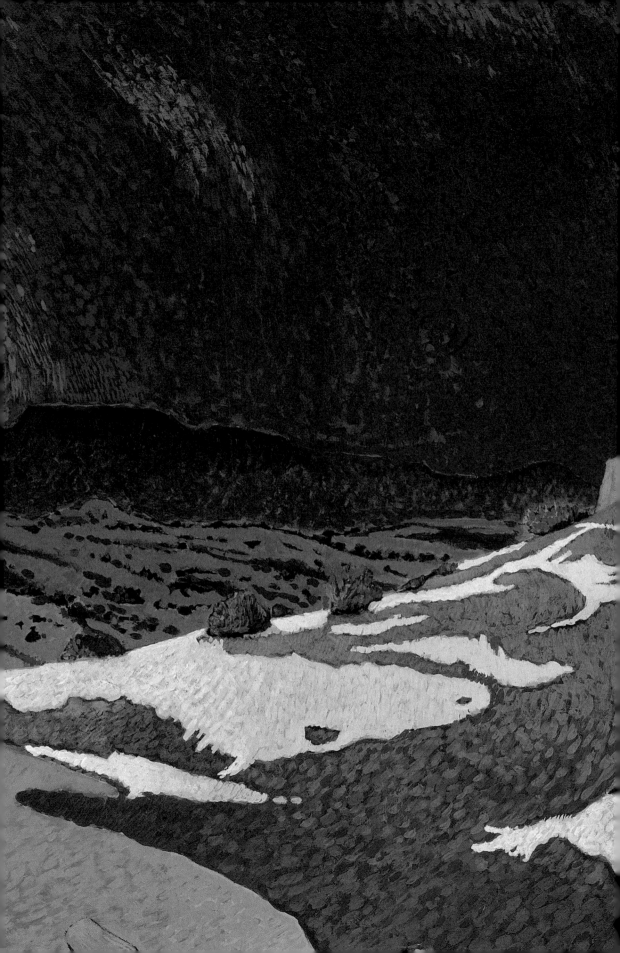

is called *chxįįdii*. Someone with evil intentions can use this power to cause harm to others.

Because of chxįįdii, Navajo people avoid contact with the dead as much as possible. In the old days, when it seemed that someone was about to die, they would be moved to a small temporary shelter outside the hogan.

Today, when someone is close to death, they are removed to the hospital. The Navajos are glad to have others take care of their deceased. However, if someone should die within a hogan, that hogan can never be occupied again. The chxįįdii that remains there may cause sickness or death in others. The body is removed, not by the eastern door but through a hole broken in the wall, and the hogan is either burned or abandoned.

MISFORTUNE HAS COME TO SOMEONE WHO

lives in this hogan; a man or woman has been afflicted. The dwelling has been emptied and swept clean. Painters bring sand and cornmeal, powdered stone and roots and flower pollen. A diviner has been consulted and comes, using his own method of seeking an answer. Some diviners are Star Gazers, some are Crystal Gazers, others are Hand Tremblers, like this man. By studying the trembling of his own hand, he makes a diagnosis and prescribes the ritual for the cure. A Singer has been contacted as well.

Four days have passed, and now the ceremony will begin. So it has been for centuries and so it is today, for within the Navajo world, whenever there is illness or bad luck, there is also a remedy, a healing Way that can be used to restore one's balance with the universe.

When the Hataałii arrives at the hogan, he has already been given a gift of cash to thank him for his work. This may be as little as $50 for a one-night sing or as much as $1,000 for a nine-day Way. Such a ceremony is a serious investment for family members, who also provide food for those additional people who come to the final days of the ceremony to provide support for the one being healed.

The Singer brings apprentice helpers with him, but it is expected that the entire family of the one who must be restored to balance will assist in every possible way. This Singer has been asked to perform the Night Chant because it is the right Way for the ailment that is to be remedied. Each of the many curing chantways is associated with a particular affliction.

No Singer has ever known all the songs or Ways. Most know only one or two, learned over a long apprenticeship to a senior Hataałii. There are, it is said, over a hundred different Ways, each incorporating hundreds of songs. The feats of memorization required to perform these oral traditions are incredible. One Way recorded by Washington Matthews included 576 songs, each of which required perfect utterance of every word and intonation to achieve its purpose. A mistake could worsen the condition of his patient or cause illness to the Singer himself.

Some Ways last three days. Others, such as the Night Chant, may take as many as nine. The Night Chant, the most frequently performed of the great ceremonies, may only be done in the seasons when the snakes are asleep and there is no danger from lightning. Like all the other Ways, it is accompanied by specific equipment, elaborate ritual and dance, and the use of herbal medicines.

The creation of a series of dry paintings, made of carefully sprinkled sand and powdered roots, bark, cornmeal, and flower pollen, is an important part of every Way. There are as many as a thousand different designs, each set associated with a different Way. These sandpaintings carefully depict the actions of the Holy People whose stories are told by the Singer as he chants the Way. Four such sandpaintings accompany the Night Chant, drawn by the singer's helpers.

On the last night of the Night Chant, the boys and girls who have reached puberty are initiated. Masked figures representing Yei, the forces of nature, appear. When these initiation ceremonies are over, the *Yé'ii bicheii* dances begin, lasting through the night. At dawn, all of the people face the east and chant the Prayer of Dawn together.

Finally, the ceremony completed, the dry paintings are swept up. The sands and powders that once shaped sacred stories are carefully gathered and carried outside by the singer. Praying, he walks to the east, the south, the west, and the north. Then he releases it all back to Earth and Sky and the four directions, where eternal harmony and sacred beauty can always be found.

FOLLOWING PAGES: Those who traveled the Long Walk would have seen Fallen Timber Ridge, a 50-mile-long line of buttes and mesas east of Gallup, New Mexico. The ridge would have been on the left as the Navajos struggled along, half starved, short of water, and driven on by soldiers who shot or abandoned some of those who were unable to keep up.

THE CHEROKEES
TO MAINTAIN BALANCE

I face the east
and breathe gently to the sun.
I am praying softly:
    I turn northward
and talk to the wind.
    I turn westward
and last to south.
            I bathe my body,
touching my face
          and the coolness of water
prays with me.
    I am reluctant to leave the cold stream
but my prayer
at least this part of it
is nearly finished
          and I go shoreward
to burn red tobacco
for the earth's new morning
for the river's new earth.

Geary Hobson (Cherokee)

Listen! O Ancient White,*
where you dwell in peace
I have come to rest.
Now let your spirit arise.
Let it be buried in your stomach,
and may your appetite never be satisfied…

O Ancient White,
put me in the successful hunting trail…

Formula for Hunting Birds
from The Sacred Formulas
of the Cherokees *(1891)*

"Ancient White" is a respectful term for the fire.

ANIYUNWIYA, THE PRINCIPAL PEOPLE, IS

what the old Cherokees called themselves. Their homeland once covered an enormous area, sprawling over present-day western North Carolina, South Carolina, northern Georgia and Alabama, Tennessee, most of Kentucky, and western Virginia and West Virginia. In geography and climate it could hardly have been more different from the desert Southwest of the Navajos.

The land rolled up from the southern Piedmont plateau into the mist-shrouded Great Smoky Mountains, where deep valleys were carved out by rushing streams. Wide deposits of fertile alluvial soil made for good farming. The forests were alive with game of all kinds, from the beaver and fox, whose pelts would later be a main trade item with Europeans, to the bear and the deer who provided food and clothing for the people.

The creatures of the forest were not seen with European eyes. The Cherokees recognized animals as sentient beings that were aware not only of themselves, but of the humans they allowed to hunt them.

Long ago, the Cherokees say, the bears were a tribe of human beings. In this time, there was not much food to hunt. So, members of the bear tribe volunteered to turn themselves into animals so the humans could hunt them and obtain food. While the animals sanctioned their own sacrifice, they expected that a balance would be kept. When it was not, there were consequences.

OPPOSITE: According to Cherokee legend, animals brought disease to humans in retribution for overhunting. In time, humans learned to hunt animals only as needed and to give thanks for the animals' sacrifice.

PAGES 80-81: The sun sets over the Cumberland Mountains in Tennessee along the Trail of Tears.

PRECEDING PAGES: Blue Blossom plays a tune on the fiddle, an instrument adopted long ago by Cherokee musicians.

One of the oldest Cherokee tales stresses the importance of keeping that balance.

In the old days, the animals, the birds, the fishes, the insects and plants lived together in peace and friendship with the people. As time went on, though, the human beings grew in number. Their settlements spread over the Earth and the animals began to suffer. The human beings had invented bows and spears, blowguns, and snares and hooks. They caught nearly all of the fish in the streams. They slaughtered the larger animals and birds for food and crushed the smaller creatures beneath their feet in contempt or carelessness. So the various animals held council to decide what they could do.

The bears met first in their council house under Kuwa'hi Mountain, the Mulberry Place. Old White Bear Chief listened to their complaints. The humans had killed their friends, eaten their flesh, and used their skins. They showed no respect and did not give thanks. Soon all of the bears would be destroyed.

"What weapons do they use to kill us?" one bear asked.

"Bow and arrows," all the others answered.

"Of what are they made?"

"The bow is made of wood. The string is made from the entrails of a bear," came the answer.

So it was proposed that they should make their own weapons to use against the humans. One bear sacrificed himself for the good of the others so that they might make bow strings. But when the bow and arrows were made it was found that the bears' claws prevented them from drawing back the string and letting it go cleanly.

"Trim my claws off," one bear said. When this was done, the arrow went straight to its mark.

Now, though, Old White Bear Chief objected. "We need our claws to climb trees and to get food," he said. "If we cut off

In this illustration of a Cherokee legend, Rabbit, the great trickster and symbol of how the weak can defeat those more physically powerful, holds the mask of a human being. In the story, Rabbit saw a man wearing a ceremonial mask. When the man put it down, Rabbit stole it, disguising himself as a human being, and went about doing mischief.

our claws we shall starve. These human weapons were not intended for us."

So it was that the council of the bears came to no decision.

It was different when the deer met in council under their chief Ah'wusti, Little Deer. They decided that they would send rheumatism to every hunter who killed a deer without asking their pardon. They sent notice of their decision to the human beings, telling them what they must do if they truly needed to kill a deer.

Now, whenever a deer has been shot by a hunter, the Little Deer comes to that spot. Little Deer is invisible to hunters. He is as swift as the wind and may never be wounded or killed. The spirit of the deer that was killed remains at the place of its death until Ah'wusti's arrival.

"Did the hunter who killed you speak the prayer to ask your forgiveness?" Little Deer asks.

If the answer is no, then Ah'wusti follows the trail of that hunter back to his lodge. He strikes him with rheumatism so that his legs may no longer carry him into the forest and his fingers may no longer draw back the bowstring.

Other creatures, seeking to revenge themselves upon the thoughtless humans, visited further diseases upon the people. The plants, however, took pity on the human beings. They decided to provide them with medicine.

So it is that every plant, from the great trees to the small mosses, may provide a cure for one or another of our human illnesses. If a Cherokee traditional doctor does not know what medicine to use for a person who is sick, the spirit of one plant or another may speak to him and offer itself as a remedy. In return, whenever plants are gathered for medicine, something must always be given in acknowledgment of that help.

Like the Navajos, the Cherokees believe in the absolute necessity of physical harmony and spiritual balance between humans and the natural world. Their image of the universe is a portrait of such balance. High above is *Galun'lati,* the Sky World, where powerful beings live. It is the domain of *Une'lanu'hi,* the Sun, a female being whose name means "the Great Apportioner." Her Earthly counterpart is the sacred fire that is the source of life. Animals also dwell in the Upper World—not those found upon the Earth, but their ancient and powerful ancestors, who may be called upon for help.

Beneath us is the Lower World, a place under the ancient waters that was here before Earth was created. It is a world, as James Mooney recorded in *Myths of the Cherokee*, "like ours in every thing—animals, plants, people—save that the seasons are different."

The swift streams flowing down from the mountains are trails leading into that Lower World. One old story tells how a man was almost swallowed on the Tennessee River by a well-known, enchanted whirlpool known as *Un'tiguhi*, Pot-in-the-Water. Looking down into its depths, he saw roof beams and people reaching up to pull him down, but the current swept him away before they could grab hold.

Spiritual elder and medicine man Jess Bluebird looks at the world with a healer's eye. He is a member of the Keetoowahs, the Oklahoma Cherokee Band made up of full-blooded Indians. Indians and non-Indians alike seek Jess Bluebird out for prayers and healings.

When anyone enters that Lower World, they must remain there, for if they return to This World, they will die within seven days.

THE PLACE WHERE WE STAND, THIS WORLD, IS

an island resting upon the primeval waters. Its earth was built from the soil brought up long ago by Water Beetle, and it hangs from the sky by cords fastened at each of the four directions.

Each of the four directions has a color related to it. East is red, the color of dawn and the bringer of health and good fortune. Its spirit power, often invoked in Cherokee magical formulas, is referred to as Red Man or Red Woman. North is blue, a color the Cherokees associate with trouble and defeat. West is black; its spirit power is called Black Man—death itself. This ominous direction is also referred to as the Darkening Land. South is white, the color of peace and happiness.

The first two Cherokees in This World were Kanati and Selu. Kanati was a hunter and ventured into the forests every morning. He

never failed to bring back game animals for food. Selu, his wife, would go each day to their granary, coming back with a basket of corn to feed their family, which consisted of that first couple and their two sons, Lodge Boy and Wild Boy.

Eventually, though they were told to remain at home, the two boys followed their father. They discovered that he kept all the game animals in a cave. When the boys opened the cave, they released all the game animals into the world, where they remain to this day. They also discovered that their mother, Selu, drew the kernels of corn from her own body. When they accused her of witchcraft, she told them to kill her and drag her body seven times across the Earth before burying her. The boys followed her instructions, and from her grave the first corn plants grew.

Just as Cherokee men, descendants of Kanati, were skilled hunters, the women, daughters of Selu, the Corn Mother, excelled in agriculture. Cherokee women took good advantage of the great stretches of arable land in the river valleys. Villages, always situated near running streams, featured large gardens planted in crops including corn,

Jess Bluebird and his brother Blue Blossom offer a prayer of thanksgiving at Healing Rock, where Blue was cured of a serious leg problem.

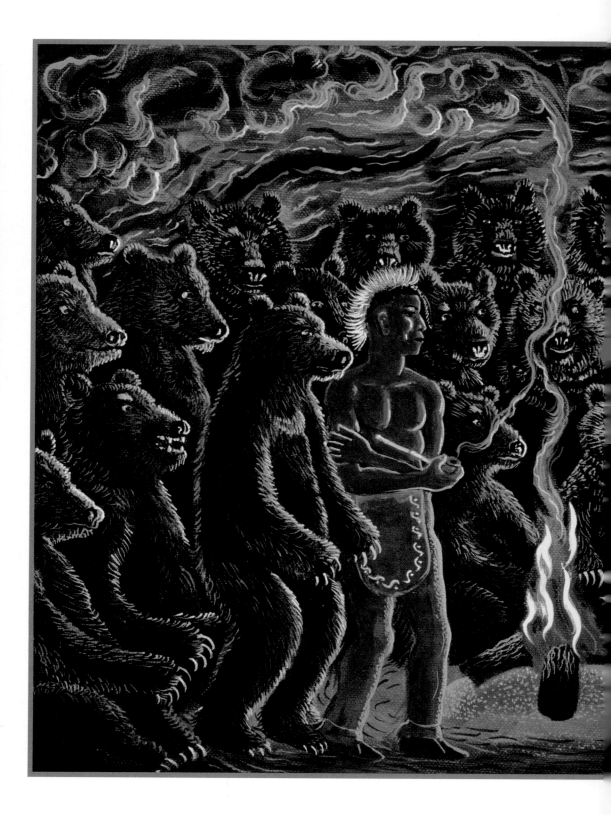

Like the Cherokees themselves, the animals are seen as nations that have leaders and council meetings for important decisions. In this scene, the Bears hold a great council to decide how to fight back against the humans.

Acorns such as these, from a variety of oak trees in eastern Tennessee, were gathered by the Cherokees, ground into flour, and then cooked. Acorns were among the increasingly scarce wild foods gathered by the thousands of hungry Cherokees on their desperate journey west.

Pat Moss, a Western
Cherokee who has been
learning medicine from the
elders, holds a medicine root
he has dug from the woods
near Tahlequah, Oklahoma.

squash, beans, and sunflowers. Men grew tobacco, the plant more important than any other for ceremonial purposes, in plots isolated from the other gardens.

The gathering of wild plants of many kinds for food and for medicine was the special responsibility of the women. Some wild plants still used to this day by the Cherokees of North Carolina include strawberries, blackberries, mulberries, huckleberries, walnuts, wild greens, persimmons, plums, grapes, mushrooms, and ginseng, as well as many other roots and herbs.

By the early 19th century, the Cherokees had begun with great success to adopt the ways of the whites, and the patterns of Cherokee agriculture had changed considerably. Though many of the same crops were still grown and there was no less reverence for Selu's gift, men took a much larger part in farming. Some Cherokee families owned huge plantations with large herds of cattle.

As among the Navajo people, Cherokee women have always been the traditional owners of the houses and the fields. The clan system, in which property and social place were inherited from the women's side only, assured the importance of women in Cherokee life. There are seven Cherokee clans: Wolf, Wild Potato, Paint, Blue, Long Hair, Bird, and Deer.

Marriage must always be with someone outside your own clan. Men and women of the same clan, even though they might share no blood connection, consider themselves related. They also feel a strong relationship to the beings which lent their names to each clan.

As Rennard Strickland, a contemporary Cherokee historian explains, his people "were guided by a deep faith in supernatural forces that linked human beings to all other living things. This belief was a common bond among all Cherokees." For the Cherokees, the term "all living things" encompasses a much larger range than it does among European Americans.

What white people refer to as forces of nature and inanimate objects are perceived by the Cherokees as aware and purposeful. Fire is centralmost among those natural forces. Yet Cherokee stories, emphasizing fire's importance, say that it was not always a part of human lives. Like the Earth itself, fire came to the people with the help of the animal beings.

In the beginning, the world was cold, for there was no fire. Then the Thunderers sent down a bolt of lightning. It made fire in the bottom of a hollow sycamore tree that grew on an island. The birds and animals saw the smoke from that fire and resolved that one of those among them who could fly or swim should go out to that island and bring it back.

The Raven was large and strong. He said that he would go and bring back fire. He flew out and landed upon that burning tree, but the heat was so great that it frightened him and his feathers were scorched and blackened. He came back without the fire.

Wahu'hu, the Screech Owl, went next. He looked down into the hollow of the burning tree and the smoke was so thick that it nearly blinded him and the white ash made rings about his eyes. He, too, came back without the fire.

Now the Little Snake swam across the water and crawled into a small hole at the bottom of the tree. But the heat was so great that it almost killed him. He barely escaped alive and his body was now all black. He became Little Black Snake. Great Snake was the next to try. He crawled up the outside of the burning sycamore tree. But it was too hot for him, also. The fire turned his body as dark as that of Little Black Snake and he became known as Great Black Snake.

Many different creatures tried to bring back the fire. None of them were successful. Almost all of those who had not already tried were too frightened to go to the island because they saw what had happened to the others.

Only Water Spider was not afraid. Water Spider spun a thread from her body and wove it into a small bowl. She placed that bowl upon her back and went across the water to the island of the burning tree. She placed a single coal in that bowl on her back and brought it back to land. So it was that Water Spider brought the fire.

Water, opposite of fire, was of equal importance in the ceremonial life of the Cherokees. The rivers and streams in particular were seen to be very much alive, as well as a link between this world and the world beneath this one. The flowing water was always addressed as *Yu'nwi Gunahi'ta,* the Long Person.

One of the most common religious practices among the Cherokee people was the purification ritual of Going to Water. This was often done just before dawn, when the river wakes up. A required ritual before ceremonies, for many people it was also something to be done every day, even in winter, when the ice on the river had to be broken. The ritual bathing helped bring good fortune, spiritual well-being, and physical health.

In the 1950s, a Cherokee elder named Da'si spoke of how he was trained from earliest childhood to be a traditional healer. "About 6 or 7 years old," he remembered, "they used to wake you up at four o'clock in the morning when the river woke up. You had to dive under and they didn't help you out. If they gave you a hand, it would make you weak. It didn't matter if it was ice. No sickness came in. I didn't have any sickness 'til 57, when I was in hospital two weeks."

To this day, despite the introduction of Christianity and the adoption of many of the visible aspects of white American culture, Going to Water remains important to many Cherokee people, and is still practiced by contemporary Cherokee "Indian doctors." It is quite likely why so many Cherokee Christians chose to join the Baptists, who practice full immersion. In the minds of many Cherokee converts, they not only have their sins washed away during the ritual: the living, listening river adds its blessing as well.

A further connection between Christian Baptism and Going to Water is the old Cherokee healing practice of speaking the patient's name while immersing the person during a curing ritual. If the cure did not work, the Cherokee healer often concluded that the river had not approved of that name. When the immersion ceremony was repeated, the healer gave the person a new name by which that man or woman would be known from then on.

THE CHEROKEE PEOPLE AS A WHOLE WERE

not an organized nation with any sort of central government until well into the 18th century. Each village was autonomous, though villages might band together to make war against a common enemy. There were four main divisions of Cherokee settlements: The Lower

OPPOSITE: Convinced that his people needed their own "talking leaves" to preserve their culture, Sequoyah began his work on a Cherokee syllabary in 1809. Each symbol in Sequoyah's alphabet stood for a syllable in spoken Cherokee. The system was so easy to master that Cherokees using it could become literate in a matter of days. Unlike English, it enabled Cherokees to write their thoughts in a fully Indian way: a horse, for example, translates as "bearer of heavy things" and a lawyer as "one who argues repeatedly."

Settlements in what is now South Carolina, the Middle Settlements of North Carolina, the Valley Settlements of Georgia and Tennessee, and the Overhill Settlements in northern Tennessee and Kentucky.

Within each village, there were essentially two different governments whose roles were in careful balance. The first was the White or Peace government, led by a seven-member Council headed by a chief or high priest. This government of older and wiser men of the tribe was supreme at all times, except during war.

When war began, the second government, the Red or War government, took control and kept it as long as the fighting continued. The Red government was made up of much younger people. Its seven officers, led by the Great Red War Chief, also included War Woman or Beloved Woman. One of her roles was to judge the fate of prisoners of war and any others taken captive.

The purpose of both governments was to ensure that the village enjoyed harmony and public consensus. Disputes or confrontations were to be avoided. In fact, if a division developed within a village and consensus could no longer be found, then those who were in disagreement with the majority would not remain as a disgruntled opposition party. They would move to another location and establish another village.

The laws of the people were not viewed as human-made civil rules, but as norms of behavior stemming directly from the divine. They were encoded into wampum belts, whose symbols were a mnemonic tool to remember the ancient precepts. The Cherokee law would be spoken once a year at the Busk or First Fruit Ceremony by Beloved Man, a tribal orator wearing the wings of a raven in his hair and holding the wampum belts in his hand.

The event was described in John Haywood's *The Natural and Aboriginal History of Tennessee*, published in 1828:

> "The great beloved man or high priest addresses the warriors and women, giving them all the particular and positive injunctions, and negative precepts they yet retain of the ancient law....He enumerates the crimes they have committed, great and small, and bids them look at the holy fire which has forgiven them."

That sacred fire was to be found at the heart of every Cherokee village and remains the central symbol of the Cherokee people. It is referred to as Ancient Red or Ancient White, names spoken to describe the fire in sacred terms and acknowledge it as a revered elder.

Fire and smoke are spirit beings, visible manifestations of those spirit forces that shape the world. Gatherings and councils took place around the fire as did the sacred dances, done in a circle around the flames. The songs sung were said to be so sacred that they could only be uttered in the presence of the fire. The fire paid close attention to all of these things.

Once a year, each village held a special ceremony called the Great Festival of the Expiation of Sins. At that festival of renewal, the divine fire was appeased for past crimes. If one asked pardon of the fire, any crime—with the exception of murder—could be forgiven after the

Suppressed for many years by those who saw it as a pagan ritual, the stomp dance was reintroduced among Western Cherokees in the early 20th century and remains an important part of Cherokee culture. Many Christian Cherokees see the stomp dance as simply another way of worshiping the same God, whose spirit— just as in the Bible—is visible in the sacred flame.

Yellow wildflowers abound in a cattle pasture east of Tahlequah, Oklahoma. In fields such as this, resourceful Cherokees reestablished their cattle herds after removal to Indian Territory.

passing of a year. Because the fire sees into the heart, no one could speak anything but the truth. Any lie would remain upon a person as a great stain, and after death they would not be able to go to the Cherokee afterlife in the Darkening Land.

The Cherokee way of seeing and interacting in the world acknowledges the interrelatedness of things and the existence of forces more powerful than human beings. Through prayer and ceremony these forces might be convinced to lend their assistance to humans.

According to the beliefs of the Cherokees as well as the Navajos, natural resources including land, game animals, and wild plants were shared by everyone. Personal wealth was not important. There was ownership of property, but also the expectation that whatever one had would be shared freely with others. Social harmony was desired above all else. Decisions affecting the village—and later, after the Cherokee people had become a political unit, the Cherokee Nation as a whole—

were to be reached by consensus. The people must be of one mind.

In 1821, Sequoyah bestowed a great gift to his people. He presented the Cherokee Nation with an alphabet he had created after more than a decade of trial and error. Using 86 symbols, each representing a spoken syllable in Cherokee, most Cherokees were were able to learn to read and write within a matter of days.

Cherokee priests (or "conjurors," as they came to be known by the late 18th century), were quick to see the usefulness of Sequoyah's gift. In addition to putting the syllabary to work for correspondence and for recording events, they began to use it to record their sacred formulas. The recitation of the powerful chanted poems, which call upon various beings and forces, is a means to focus those energies, much the way a magnifying glass can be used to concentrate the rays of the sun.

These sacred formulas were used for many purposes. In 1887 and 1888, pioneering ethnologist John Mooney collected formulas from the manuscripts of such North Carolina Cherokee Indian doctors as Ayuh ini (Swimming as a Snake Swims), Gatigwanasti (Belt), Inali (Black Fox), and Gahuni. He catalogued their uses "covering every subject pertaining to daily life and thought of the Indian, including medicine, love, hunting, fishing, war, self-protection, destruction of enemies, witchcraft, the council, the ball play, etc., and, in fact, embodying almost the whole of the ancient religion of the Cherokees."

The Cherokee ball game noted by Mooney illustrates how Cherokee lives have always connected with the spirit world around them. According to Jerry Wolf, a respected Cherokee elder and maker of the sticks used in Indian ball, the game teaches important values such as spiritual balance, cooperation, and inclusion. It also reaffirms much of what it means to be Cherokee. Played between townships until well into the 20th century, Indian ball involved a lot of preparation. While the teams practiced, the Indian doctor prepared the medicines he was going to use.

The night before the game, the townspeople gathered wood and built a fire along the river they called Long Person, from which they gathered strength. The Indian doctor, meanwhile, built a fire for the players. He would light it and turn toward the opponent's home town and yell lah-ehlah, Cherokee for "woodpecker pecking on a tree." Like a bird pecking, then listening for the worm, the Indian doctor called out into the night and listened to hear if the ball spirit would answer. Then he gave the signal for the dance to begin. While the townspeople watched, the players held their ball sticks in their hands as they danced around the fire.

In time, all the players lined up by the river, and the Indian doctor called on the spirits using rituals and chants. He used beads to foretell the results of the coming game—black beads for the opposing team, and red beads for his own. The beads were placed on a wooden peg the Indian doctor had driven into the ground, and the losing color was the one that fell off.

Seven times in the night they went down to the river. As the Sun came up, the Indian doctor sowed the beads in the Earth and asked the women to dance over them and stomp their opponents into the ground. At last they made their way to the playing field, stopping three times along the way. During the game, whenever a player scored, he took a sip of medicine from a bucket by the field.

In their own game, the animals, ancient guides and teachers, remind humans of the balance we need to maintain. Long ago, the story goes, the animals of the forest had two ball teams. Wolf, Fox, Panther, Bobcat, and Deer were on the vicious team, and Great Bear was their captain. The birds had their own team, which included Falcon, Hawk, Crow, Raven, Kingfisher, and Hummingbird. Eagle was their captain.

The Bear boasted that no team could ever beat his, certainly not the bird team, and to underscore his point he picked up and tossed large boulders and logs. Meanwhile someone tapped him on his toe, trying to get his attention. It was Mouse who looked up and said, "I came to join your team and to play ball with you tomorrow."

The Bear laughed so hard he fell down. He asked little Mouse: "What can you do in a ball game? Look who you are."

I'm an animal," said Mouse, "and this is an animal game." And the Bear kicked him into the bushes. The Mouse walked for miles through the forest to ask Eagle if he could join his team.

Eagle said he was welcome, but he needed wings. So he found a piece of leather and asked Kingfisher, who had a beak as sharp as scissors, to cut a set of wings for the little mouse. Eagle carried him high up and dropped him from the sky. Mouse fluttered down, back and forth, back and forth, but he was flying.

In the game, the Mouse grabbed the ball and darted in and out through the animals and scored again and again to win the game. Indian doctors still warn against underestimating the size of someone and what they can do. Always accept him on your team, they say, because if you don't he'll get ahead of you.

To this day, if we look up into the sky in the evening, we may see the bat, that little Mouse with wings, fluttering around up there to remind us.

BEFORE THE COMING OF THE WHITE MEN,

an *Ada'wehi,* a Cherokee healer whose supernatural powers are great, has been visited by a hunter who has been troubled by the stiffness in his hands and legs. His malady is a sign of the feared *Didunles'ki,* "the crippler," the rheumatism brought upon a human being by an offended game animal.

The hunter has brought the Ada'wehi a fine deerskin as the *usista'ti,* the ritual gift for the Cherokee healer. It is not payment as we know it, but an offering to the disease spirit itself. It also serves as a covering to protect the hand of the healer as he draws the sickness out of his patient.

Well before the curing ceremony, the Ada'wehi has work that must be done. He must gather medicines from the forest. He does so with great care, for the plants are aware not only of his presence, but even his thoughts. Were his mind filled with anger or jealousy, they would hide from him. *I am small and weak,* he sings softly as he walks, *so I come to you for help.*

Though this man knows in his heart that his own powers are great, he never allows himself to be caught by the snares of pride. He remembers, as do all his people, what happened long ago to the *Ani'kuta'ni,* the clan of priests who once controlled all of the sacred ceremonies. They grew so haughty that they abused their power, treating others as servants, taking women from their husbands. Finally the people could stand it no longer. They rose up and all of the Ani'kuta'ni were killed.

There, on the moist floor of the forest, he sees one of the plants for which he has been searching. It is *Utistugi*—Solomon's Seal. From

its root, he can make a poultice to treat bruising. The man who has come to him for help suffers not only from the rheumatism which has made his fingers stiff, but also from bruises he sustained in a fall. Even though this is the plant he seeks, the Ada'wehi passes it by. He must see at least three others of the same plant before he begins to take even one.

There are other rules he must follow to make certain his medicines are potent. For example, when he takes bark from a tree or part of any plant's root, he must always do so from the eastern side, for that is the side which absorbs the healing strength of the sunrise.

As the Ada'wehi walks slowly through the woods, his eyes take

in the hundreds of other plants that provide medicine. There is *A'tali Kuli*, the "one that climbs the mountain" —ginseng. The tea made from its root will help with headaches or cramps. There is *Yana Utsesta*, the "one Bear lies on"—the shield fern. It is another of the plants he has come to gather. He will use it along with *Ka'ga Skuntagi*, "crow's shin"—maidenhair fern—and two other smaller ferns.

He begins collecting the maidenhair fern, for there is much of it here. He will not take the largest ones, for they are the parents of this family. Having chosen the plants he will take, the Ada'wehi is careful in his approach, walking around each fern four times in a sunwise direction, reciting prayers that ask for help. Then, kneeling, he speaks

J.T. Garrett prays to the sacred flowing water the Cherokees call Long Person along this stream near the Qualla Boundary in North Carolina. An apprentice to a traditional Cherokee medicine man, he is also health director for Carteret County on the North Carolina coast.

to each plant before he removes it, explaining his purpose and giving thanks for its sacrifice. As he does this, he drops one red or black bead into each hole left by the roots, and covers it with earth.

The sun has only moved the width of one hand across the sky by the time all of the medicine plants that he needs have been gathered. But he is not yet ready to return home. He takes the package of plants he has gathered and walks down to the stream bank. Once again he chants his prayers. This time he asks the Long Person for guidance and help. May it show him that these medicines are the right ones, that his treatment will be successful.

Then he casts the bundle of medicines into the water. He holds his breath as he does so. If the carefully gathered bundle should sink, he has made some crucial mistake and must start over again or his treatment will fail. But the Long Person must approve of what he has done thus far, for the bundle bobs on top of the gentle current. With a smile on his face, the Ada'wehi walks downstream and then wades in, allowing the Long Person to float the medicine plants into his outstretched palms.

In the morning, well before dawn, the Ada'wehi again stands by the flowing stream. His patient, the ailing hunter, is beside him. The two naked men glow with heat, and steam rises from the pores of their skin in the cool air, for they have just stepped out of the sweat lodge dug into the nearby hillside.

The intense heat within that small earth-covered structure has drawn streams of sweat from their bodies. The air is thick to the point of choking, not only from the heat, but from the medicinal steam created when water filled with the pulverized roots of wild parsnip was poured over the glowing stones.

Through it all, the Ada'wehi has been speaking, chanting, and singing. His words are addressed to the sickness itself and to the powers that will help him. "Sge!" he calls out. "Listen!"

Sge! Ha! In the Sun land you repose, O Red Dog,
O you have swiftly drawn near to hearken.
O Great Ada'wehi, you never fail in anything.
O appear, and draw near running, for your prey never escapes.

You are now come to remove the intruder.
Ha! You have settled a very small part of it
Far off there at the end of the earth…

His recitation of the sacred formula continues as he takes a small flint arrowhead and scratches it on the afflicted limbs of his patient. With his other hand he rubs into the scratches one of the medicines he prepared before dawn. Carefully boiled together, the medicine was waiting, still warm, in a clay bowl by the stream bank. Next to it is a terrapin shell which holds a small part of the medicine and two white beads. The medicine in the terrapin shell is for the helping spirits and is not to be used on the ailing man. The Ada'wehi's strong fingers are now at work on the man's limbs, massaging out the disease, massaging in strength.

Then it is time to Go to Water. The Ada'wehi leads his patient into a deep part of the stream and immerses him completely beneath the water seven times. They repeat the ritual three more times: once when the Sun is on the horizon, again when the Sun is three hands high, and lastly, when the Sun is at its greatest height in the sky. Then the ritual is done.

The man who has been cured may now eat after a day of fasting, but he must still observe certain practices. He must remain in a special bark lodge constructed for him some distance from the village. There, for the next four days, he must sit in a seat reserved only for him and avoid contact with his wife or his dogs. But as he enters the bark lodge, his spirit has been lifted, for the pains that troubled him have left his limbs.

Was it the heat of the sweat, the herbal medicines, the massaging of the Ada'wehi's strong fingers, or the powerful chanted formulas that affected this cure?

The hunter and the Ada'wehi do not question that it was all of these things. They are all part of those ancient traditions that have always helped the Principal People to live in This World.

As long as the people maintain this sacred balance, all will go well for them in their homeland, the place that gives both life and health to the Cherokees.

FOLLOWING PAGES:
Near these waters, Cherokees were held at the Fort Cass Emigrating Depot before making their western journey on the Trail of Tears. Today this spring waters cattle on a private ranch.

LEWIS
SON OF
WILLIAM P. & MARY J.
ROSS
BORN APRIL 19, 1852
DIED APRIL 3, 1853

Formula To Destroy Life

Sge! Listen! Now I have come to step
    over your soul.
You are of the (wolf) clan. Your name is A'yuh ini.
Your spittle I have placed at rest under the earth.
I have come to cover you over with
    the black rock.
I have come to cover you over with
    the black cloth.
I have come to cover you over with
    the black slabs,
      never to reappear…

> *written by Ayuh ini*
> *from* The Sacred Formulas of the Cherokees

They said among themselves, "What did we
do wrong?" We people here didn't do any harm.
We were gathered up for no reason. The ones
that were doing all the killing and raiding of the
White Men probably are still doing the same
thing back home—raiding and stealing from the
White Men and killing. We harmless people are
held here, and we want to go back to our lands
right away.

> *Howard Gorman*
> *from* Navajo Stories of
> the Long Walk Period

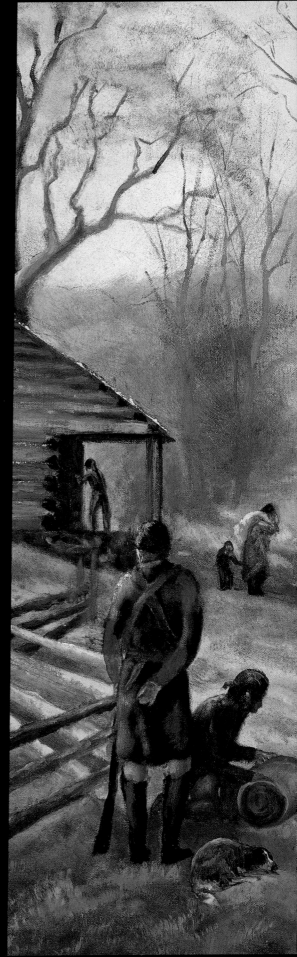

A DEEP SNOW HAS FALLEN, AND CLOUDS OF
breath shroud the faces of men and horses as their column forms in front of Fort Canby in the Arizona Territory. It is January 6, 1864. The fort is in the Navajo heartland, a short march from the Navajo strong-hold of Canyon de Chelly. The first fort in this place was christened Fort Defiance, but the white soldiers have their own name for this place—Hell's Gate.

At the head of the column is Kit Carson, the man known to many Navajos as "Rope-Thrower" for his legendary skills with a lasso. He is about to tighten his noose about their nation. Carson's men and the soldiers who will follow them over the next year will lay Dinetah to waste, burning homes and fields of corn and wheat, destroying stores of food, girdling peach trees, killing more Navajos by starvation than with bullets. His Ute Indian scouts look forward to taking many Nava-jos captive and selling them as slaves to Mexicans.

Over this year and the next, the Navajo people will stagger into the forts in great numbers, their clothing tattered, their children and elders dying, their eyes filled with tears at the thought of leaving this beloved land. No pity will be shown to them, for the orders given to Carson in 1863 by Gen. James H. Carleton are explicit: "Say to them, Go to the Bosque Redondo or we will pursue and destroy you. We will not make peace with you on any other terms. You have deceived us too often and robbed and murdered our people too long to trust

OPPOSITE: Its deep grooves spreading like the branches of a tree, this rock was once used to melt pine pitch used to lubricate wheel axles. Such rocks have been found in a number of places along the Cherokees' Trail of Tears. Near this place in the woods south of Spencer, Tennessee, the trail's deep ruts are still visible.

PAGES 110-111: The head-stone of a child's grave in the Ross family cemetery bears silent witness to the hard life the Cherokees faced in their new lands.

PRECEDING PAGES: The Cherokees mount wagons as they begin their journey on Nunda ut sungi, the Place Where We Cried.

you again at large in your own country. This war shall be pursued against you if it take years, now that we have begun, until you cease to exist or move. There can be no other talk on the subject."

These words about robbery and murder applied more to the actions of whites than to those of the Navajos. In the years since Gen. Stephen W. Kearney claimed New Mexico from the Spanish by right of conquest in 1846, the Navajos had been more often the deceived than the deceivers. More Navajos had been killed than white men, gunned down like their elderly chief Narbona while in the midst of negotiations for peace. Thousands of Navajos remained slaves in the hands of the Mexicans and New Mexicans as part of the trade in Indian lives that had sparked Navajo resistance for 250 years. No one knows what Kit Carson thought of his mission as his troops set out into the white cold of that winter morning with this song:

Come dress your ranks my gallant souls, a standing in a row.
Kit Carson he is waiting to march against the foe.
At night we march to Moqui, o'er lofty hills of snow,
To meet and crush the savage foe, bold Johnny Navajo
Johnny Navajo, O Johnny Navajo,
We'll first chastise, then civilize, bold Johnny Navajo.

It was not the first time that the United States had sent its armies on the march to drive an entire native nation from its land.

BY 1838, THE CHEROKEE NATION, WHICH once extended over much of the southeastern United States, had been constricted to a small circle where the corners of the states of Georgia, Tennessee, North Carolina, and Alabama came together. Here, Cherokees lived and dressed much as did their white neighbors. Their homes were neatly kept, ranging from log cabins and modest structures with white picket fences lined with hollyhocks and roses to great

Legendary Indian fighter Kit Carson was the hero of dime novels in his day. He had been Indian agent for the Utes, who served as his scouts during the campaign against the Navajos. This photograph was taken in December 1864, less than a year after he completed his brutal scorched-earth campaign that broke the Navajo Nation and sent more than 9,000 people into exile at Bosque Redondo.

plantations with herds of cattle and fine horses. Despite their losses, the 16,000 Cherokees still fought—not in the woods, but in the courts—to prevent their removal. Principal Chief John Ross took their case as far as the U.S. Supreme Court.

But the enemies of the Cherokees were implacable. The state of Georgia threatened to secede from the Union if all the Indians of the South were not removed west of the Mississippi River. Even though the Supreme Court had ruled in favor of the Cherokee people, and the Treaty of New Echota which agreed to their removal had been signed by only a handful of Cherokees with no legal right to act for their nation, the fatal hour had come. New forts were built, some of them on the sites of church-run schools that once taught Cherokee children arithmetic and grammar, history and Latin. The Cherokees were to be held at such sites before they were transported west.

In May 1838, Gen. Winfield Scott was in charge of an army of U.S. Regulars and Militia Volunteers that was headquartered in New Echota, once the thriving capital of the Cherokee Nation. "Old Fuss and Feathers," as his men fondly called Scott, had cleared the Indians from the Cherokee courthouse, the schools, and the building that housed the *Cherokee Phoenix,* the Cherokee Nation's own newspaper. His predecessor, Gen. Elias Wool, resigned before him because he was unwilling to carry out the orders he regarded as a great injustice to humanity.

As ten thousand troops fanned out across the Cherokee Nation, doors were broken down and the air was shattered by the sounds of horses' hooves and the soldiers' rough curses and gunshots. No shots were fired from Cherokee guns. The Indians did not try to fight back. Their leaders, especially Principal Chief John Ross, told them not to resist. As their homes were ransacked by white looters following the troops, as smoke filled the air from burning barns and houses, stunned Cherokees grabbed the few possessions they could carry—sometimes only a blanket or a book—before they were forced to stumble ahead of the bayonets leveled at their backs.

Impeccably dressed as he always was on the many trips made to Washington to forestall removal, John Ross shows his determination in this portrait. Fondly called Tsan Usdi, or Little John, by his devoted followers, he was small in stature but great in spirit. He served as Principal Chief of the Cherokee Nation, first in his homeland and then in the new Indian settlement, through the most turbulent years of its history.

Though more than a century and a half has passed since the exiled Cherokees came along this route just south of Spencer, Tennessee, the deeply worn section of the Trail of Tears remains. Today the path is used by hunters and hikers, many of whom do not know whose weary feet trod there before them.

"The Cherokees," General Scott told the army of removal in his orders of May 17th, "by the advances they have made in Christianity and civilization are by far the most interesting tribe of Indians in the territorial limits of the United States....Every possible kindness must, therefore, be shown by the troops."

Despite Scott's orders, there was little gentleness in that night and the days that followed. People were beaten and killed as elders fell by the roadside on their way to the camps. Not all were dragged from their homes; some came in willingly.

As efficient as it was brutal, the roundup of Cherokees was complete in less than three weeks. On June 17 General Scott dismissed his volunteer soldiers, leaving army regulars to guard the concentration camps. There were 9,000 held in Calhoun, Tennessee, 2,000 at Gunstocker Spring, and 1,600 at Mouse Creek. More than 15,000 Cherokees, according to military reports for July 1838, were held and readied for forced emigration.

How did it come to this, for the Cherokees who sought to follow their ancient paths of balance and for the Navajos whose Holy People had taught them that the way of life was to walk in beauty? The roads that led to these points of no return were marked by brutal conflict between the inexorable growth of a new America and the native nations that stood in its path.

IF SUCCESSFUL ADAPTATION IN THE FACE OF almost unimaginable change is a measure of a culture's viability, then the Cherokees and Navajos may have been the two strongest native cultures in America by the early 19th century. They were able to endure centuries of conflict with European newcomers who had laid claim to their lands and enslaved their people, and both Indian nations had found new ways that appeared to lead to the survival of their cultures. Both had grown and even prospered as they adopted certain aspects of European culture.

The Cherokees became known as the most "civilized" tribe, a people who embraced the outward trappings of American civilization as it pushed in on them from every direction. By the 19th century, Cherokee leadership concluded it was their only way to preserve what was left of their former homeland and protect their identity. But it was not a decision reached quickly.

Of all the southeastern nations, none had been more feared in war than the Cherokees. Even the colonial powers of France, Spain, and England found it difficult to contend with them. However, a series of events beginning in the mid-18th century—when the English invaded their country and destroyed their Lower Towns—convinced many Cherokees that making war against the whites was like trying to hold back the tide.

During the American Revolution, some Cherokees sided with the British, whose policy was to limit white settlements west of the Appalachians. As a result, North Carolina troops ravaged the Cherokee Middle Towns. After the Revolution, the only Cherokees still at war with the Americans were the Chickamaugas. From their lands in northeastern Alabama, aided by the Spanish and led by Chief Bloody Fellow, John Watts, and Bob Benge, they attacked white settlements.

The Treaty of Tellico Blockhouse in 1794 brought an end to the Cherokees' armed resistance. Never again would the Cherokees take up arms against the United States. They refused to join Tecumseh, the brilliant Shawnee war chief, who sought to unite all the tribes in a

*Its door open as if to welcome its owner back home, the cabin of
Hair Conrad, an influential Cherokee leader and key member of the
Cherokee National Council, still stands. Born in 1780, Hair Conrad
was leader of the First Detachment of Cherokees heading west on
the Trail of Tears. He fell ill and died soon after reaching the new
Indian lands. The cabin, on a farm near Cleveland, Tennessee,
was built in 1800 from split-and-hewn oak and poplar logs.*

Though most graves along the Trail of Tears have been hidden by the passage of time, a plaque marks the resting place of Otahki Bushyhead. "Princess" Otahki died following the crossing of the Mississippi River, a mile east of this spot. The well-visited grave is within Trail of Tears State Park just north of Cape Girardeau, Missouri.

great alliance to drive out the Americans during the War of 1812.

Yet the warrior spirit still lived in the Cherokees. It showed itself during the War of 1812, when Gen. Andrew Jackson was unable to find white troops for his campaign against the Red Stick Creeks. Jackson's first major recruits were Cherokee volunteers. Among the 500 Cherokee soldiers were prominent figures in Cherokee history including Major Ridge, John Ross, and Sequoyah. Were it not for the Cherokees—one fourth of his army at the time—Jackson's great victory on March 27, 1814 at Horseshoe Bend might have been a defeat.

Another factor that changed Cherokee destiny was an invisible one—infectious diseases brought from Europe. Throughout the 18th century, the Cherokees were more weakened by smallpox than by force of arms. In 1738, half of the Cherokee population died in an epidemic carried by white traders. Every traditional remedy, from sweat baths to immersion in the stream, failed. Even Ancient Red and the Long Person were powerless against this new malady. Cherokee priests lost prestige in the eyes of their people and lost faith in themselves. By the end of the 18th century, the equilibrium of the Cherokees had been deeply shaken.

In the 1790s, a series of events began to occur that would shape a new way. A class of merchant Cherokees emerged, many of them of mixed blood—children of white traders and Cherokee mothers. These were men who understood not just the language but also the psychology of the whites. At the same time, white missionaries were setting up mission schools throughout the Cherokee lands. Though most Cherokees did not wish to convert to Christianity, they were eager for the knowledge these schools gave them, knowledge to tip the balance in favor of Cherokee survival. Missionaries including Samuel Worcester, Daniel Butrick, and Elizur Butler proved not only to be excellent teachers, they also devoted their lives and their honor to the defense of the Cherokees they grew to know, love, and respect. When the Cherokees were sent west, the white missionaries and their families went with them as doctors, helpers, and fellow sufferers.

By the start of the 19th century, more than 16,000 Cherokees occupied an area that amounted to less than one quarter of their former territory. A new law was enacted by the Cherokee Nation to prevent the transfer of what land was left. Any Cherokee who sold land to the whites without the agreement of the Cherokee Nation would be punished by death. In 1807, Chief Doublehead, who leased land to white men, suffered that penalty. Major Ridge was one of his executioners.

A sense of a unified Cherokee political identity began to develop. Taking the United States as a model, they transformed their political structure from a loose union of villages to a nation under a single executive. Following the suggestion of President Thomas Jefferson, the Cherokee people became a nation of citizen farmers similar in outward dress and culture to the whites around them.

A number of Cherokees adopted another aspect of southeastern white culture—the practice of black slavery. Though most Indians saw slavery as an unfortunate institution at best, the wealthier Cherokees, including the Ridges and Rosses, had as many African slaves on their plantations as did their white neighbors.

As the Cherokees were moving toward modern nationhood, Sequoyah presented his people with his ingenious syllabary. Soon the laws of the newly organized nation were written down—in both English and Cherokee.

In 1825, the Cherokee government voted to establish its own printing press and newspaper in their capital, New Echota. The man

Harvested cornfields such as this one near Hopkinsville, Kentucky, were a typical sight along the Trail of Tears as the Cherokees passed this way in the fall of 1838. Food was so scarce for the exiles that although John Ross's brother Lewis purchased corn and other supplies along the way, the travelers often had to rely on the generosity of farmers.

Changing leaves mark the coming of frost in Pennysville State Resort Park near Dawson Springs, Kentucky. This forest, a few miles north of the Trail of Tears, was typical of those scoured for game by Cherokee hunters equipped with bows, arrows, and blowguns.

chosen to raise money for the press and to edit the newspaper was a full-blood Cherokee born with the name Gallegina Watie. A graduate of the American Mission Board schools, he had been sent to the Foreign Mission School in Cornwall, Connecticut, to continue his education. There, upon meeting the head of the American Bible Study, Elias Boudinot, he took the old Bible scholar's name to honor him. On February 1, 1828, young Elias Boudinot published the first issue of the *Cherokee Phoenix*, its name and symbol drawn from the legendary Egyptian bird that rises reborn from its own ashes. It so suited Cherokee philosophy that many Cherokees believe to this day that the phoenix is an ancient Cherokee myth.

By 1827 a Cherokee government had been formed with a constitution, a legislature with two houses, a supreme court, and an executive branch with a Principal Chief and a Deputy Principal Chief—William Hicks and John Ross, respectively. The following year, the General Council elected John Ross Principal Chief by a vote of 36 to 4. Ross held the position for 38 years, never losing an election.

Even as the Cherokees took this new path, their "civilized" ways widely praised by many influential whites, the seeds of their removal had already been sown.

In 1802, the state of Georgia had already ceded its western lands to the United States in exchange for extinguishing all Indian land titles in the Southeast. Over the years, so much pressure was put on the Cherokees to leave that a number of Cherokee emigrations to Arkansas had already taken place. Doublehead's death in 1807 spurred the migration of over 1,000 Cherokees from the Lower Towns with 30 or more of their black slaves under Doublehead's brother, Chief Tahlonteskee. These Cherokees, and others who followed over the next two decades, formed a separate western Cherokee government and became known as the Old Settlers.

In 1828, running on a platform of Indian Removal, Andrew Jackson was elected President of the United States. In the following year gold was discovered on Cherokee lands in Georgia, and laws were passed that made it illegal for Cherokees to dig for gold on their own land. A Georgia Guard was created to control the gold rush that ensued. Cherokee County was created out of Indian lands, and the division of Cherokee properties by state lottery was begun.

In 1830 the infamous Indian Removal Bill passed by the narrowest of margins in the U. S. Congress. Over the next ten years, as many as 80,000 Indians were removed west of the Mississippi to what is now eastern Oklahoma. The Five Civilized Tribes—Cherokee, Creek, Choctaw, Chickasaw, and Seminole—were the main peoples targeted for removal, but more than 60 native nations were removed to Oklahoma, including the Shawnee, Kickapoo, and Delaware.

The Cherokees fought their removal in the courts, finding many allies among both ordinary and famous citizens. Prominent white political figures, from Sam Houston and Senator David (Davy) Crockett to former President John Quincy Adams spoke passionately in defense of the Cherokees. Petitions were signed in New England towns. Scores of editorials urged that the Cherokees be allowed to remain in their homes. Through it all, the Cherokee leadership, especially Chief John Ross and other educated men such as Elias Boudinot and John Ridge, shuttled back and forth between Washington and New Echota, pursuing their cause in Congress and in the courts. Boudinot's editorials in the *Cherokee Phoenix* defended their rights with eloquence and

FOLLOWING PAGES: A barge passes easily up the Mississippi River, which once proved so great a barrier to the Cherokees. Winter ice cut off ferry traffic, stranding parties for weeks on the eastern shore. This aerial view looks south with Missouri's Trail of Tears State Park on the right. To the left is Illinois. The barge is near the point of one of the old ferry crossings.

125

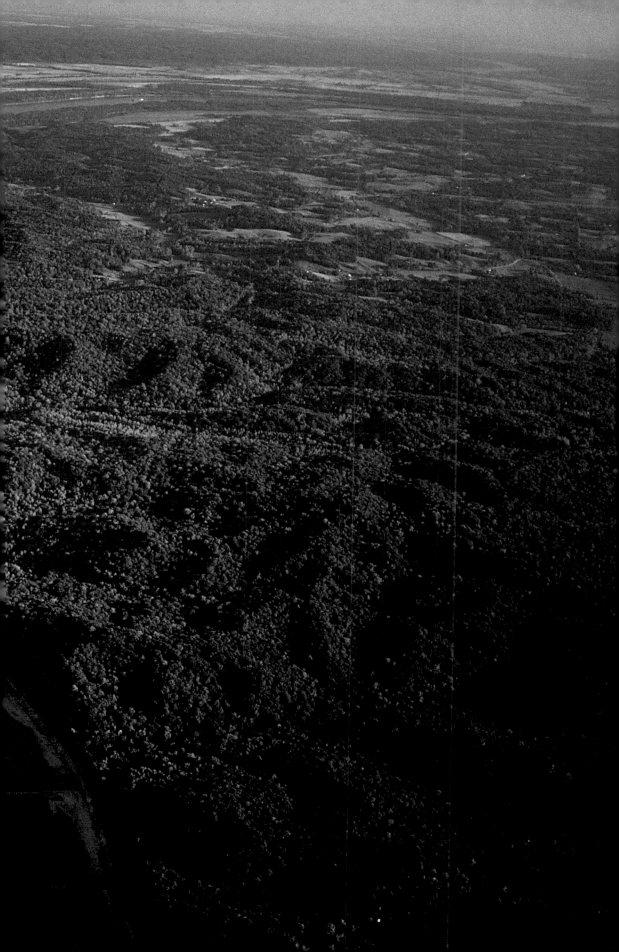

irony. Chief John Ross and his council turned down one offer after another for the lands of the Cherokees. No Cherokee, Chief Ross said, would prepare for removal.

John Ross spoke for the great majority of his people, whose determination to remain in their homeland was as deep and strong as their flowing rivers. But Georgia state government was inflexible. Though the Supreme Court ruled in 1831 that the laws of Georgia were inferior to those of the United States in the case of the Cherokees, that decision was not enforced.

"The Constitution, the laws and treaties of the United States are prostrate in the state of Georgia," wrote John Quincy Adams in his diary. "The Union is in the most imminent danger of dissolution." In fact, dissolution was another three decades away, but the deep and conflicting emotions brought to the surface in the American nation by the brutality of Indian removal presaged the eventual Civil War.

By 1832, with the exception of a few remaining Seminoles in Florida waging a guerrilla war in the impenetrable swamps, every other visible Indian nation but the Cherokees had been removed from the Southeast. Concluding that

Early frost on the petals of flowers east of Frederickstown, Missouri, was a harbinger of the hardships the Cherokees would face. The onset of winter in 1838 fell hard on the Cherokees. Short of blankets and winter clothing and without adequate tents, many suffered or died from frostbite and pneumonia.

removal could not be forestalled, a small group of Cherokees broke with John Ross. Led by Major Ridge, John Ridge, Stand Watie, and Elias Boudinot, they formed their own treaty party. Boudinot resigned as editor of the *Cherokee Phoenix*, which struggled to bring out a few more issues under other editorship. The last edition was published in 1834, shortly before the press was seized by the Georgia Guard.

Even before a treaty was signed, the seizure of Cherokee property in Georgia was in full swing. In April 1835 John Ross came home from Washington to find that his house and plantation in Georgia had been taken over by white lottery winners, his wife and children evicted. He paid as a common lodger to spend the night in his own home, then set out for the Cherokee meeting grounds in Red Clay, where the Cherokee capital had been relocated due to the loss of New Echota.

Among the friends and defenders of John Ross and the Cherokees was the composer John Howard Payne. The Cherokees had invited him to write a history of their people, hoping to use it to sway public opinion. Payne interviewed Cherokee elders, collecting information about Cherokee history and customs and every aspect of their ancient ways into a large manuscript. The more he learned, the more respect he had for these remarkable people.

On December 5, while he and John Ross were on their way to Washington, the two men were taken captive by the Georgia Guard and held prisoner at Fort Benton, the former Springplace Mission Station. At one point during the 13 days they were held, their jailer began humming Payne's own "Home Sweet Home," by then a well-loved favorite. Thinking to strike up a conversation and obtain some information about their prospects, Payne told the jailer he was the song's author. The jailer's response was a rough curse and another chorus.

It was probably no accident that Ross's mission to Washington was delayed. Jackson's prime negotiator for removal, the Reverend John F. Schermerhorn, had planned a meeting at New Echota for the signing of a removal treaty with the anti-Ross party. Schermerhorn was viewed with disdain by other Christian ministers and Cherokees alike. The Cherokee nickname for him was 'Sgina' Yona, which means "Devil's Horn."

Fewer than one hundred Cherokees came to his treaty meeting, which convened on December 22. The 20 Cherokees designated to discuss the treaty's terms included Ross's major opponents: Major Ridge, John Ridge, Elias Boudinot, Stand Watie, and Ross's own brother, Andrew. At one point, as the treaty was being read, the roof of the building caught fire. Proof, one Cherokee bystander said, of "the indignation of Heaven at the unlawful proceedings within." Fire notwithstanding, the treaty was signed on December 29.

The signers of the Treaty of New Echota would be among the first to be escorted west by the U.S. Army, traveling by flatboat down the Tennessee River in 1837. Though many Cherokees had invoked the law of blood, saying that Ridge and Watie and Boudinot and the others must die for selling Cherokee lands, John Ross stood firm against such vengeance.

A petition protesting the illegal treaty and bearing the names of

14,000 Cherokees was presented to Congress within a matter of months, but it was ignored. There would be no turning back. Although heroic efforts by John Ross and the Cherokee leadership would delay the inevitable for another 15 months, the order for the troops to begin their roundup was finally given. On May 26, 1838 the Cherokee people took the first terrible steps on the Trail of Tears as they were torn from their homes and herded like cattle into stockades.

Although much has been written—often inaccurately—about the overland journey of the Cherokees to Fort Gibson and the new Indian lands, little has been said about their long summer of confinement in the camps. In dozens of cramped stockades, behind 12-foot-high walls, the young and the old were penned outdoors in the boiling sun with only makeshift shelters. Few had been able to gather more than a couple of possessions. A lack of sanitation, poor or inadequate food delivered by corrupt white contractors, an army ill equipped to deal with the needs of so many, all produced situations of awful squalor. At least 2,500 Cherokees perished in the stockades. Many who perished during the western emigration were children and elders weakened to near-death by their stay in these concentration camps.

John Ross arrived back from his meetings in Washington with the secretary of war to find his nation imprisoned. He had successfully presented the case that his people would be unprepared to move until the fall. A stay of the roundup order had been dispatched to General Scott. But the order took too long to reach Old Fuss and Feathers. Scott was not about to release the Cherokees he had brought in with such efficiency. They would remain in the camps, no matter what.

White and Indian Christian preachers were true angels of mercy in the camps. The Reverend Elizur Butler, a missionary from New England, and his wife cared as well as they could for the ailing. One of their own children died of a fever in the camps. The Reverend Jesse Bushyhead, a Cherokee Baptist minister, held Sunday services through it all. He and Stephen Foreman, another Cherokee preacher, even constructed a small chapel for the Christian Indians—whose numbers grew in the camps and on the trail. The old ways of healing were also being practiced by Cherokee priests. They gathered what herbs they could from the forest for medicine. The food plants gathered by Cherokee women supplemented a diet that was both inadequate and strange

OPPOSITE: On the final leg of their exhausting journey, thirsty Cherokees drank from the waters of McMurtry Spring along present-day Highway 37 in Missouri. The spring, on private land, feeds a small stream.

FOLLOWING PAGES: Like a promise of rest, early morning light filters through the mist hanging above the waters of the Illinois River. This was the last river crossing on the "Ross Route" of the Trail of Tears before reaching the new lands in Oklahoma.

to the Cherokees. In place of corn they were given white flour, which they tried to boil into a thin soup. In place of fresh meat they received salt pork, which made them sick.

On June 6, 1838, removals of the captured Cherokees began. Eight hundred Cherokees led by Lieutenant Deas were loaded into six flatboats and taken through rapids as far as Decatur. There the river was too low for them to continue by water, and they were forced to board a train. Whiskey traders flocked like vultures around the Cherokees. There was much drunkenness as the disheartened emigrants sought to drown their sorrows in alcohol. Other Cherokees attempted to flee back to the East at every possible opportunity. By the time Lieutenant Deas reached the new Indian lands, only 489 people remained.

The second group of 875 Cherokees departed on June 13, led by Lt. R.H.K. Whiteley. These Cherokees refused to accept food or clothing from the Army. Twenty-five escaped before the steamer reached Muscle Shoals. By now the river was so low that they could not even reach Decatur. They began to travel overland by wagon. Many became sick; soon as many as five people a day were dying. Only 602 survived the dry, dusty journey.

By the time the third group, led by Gen. Nathaniel Smith, was ready to leave on June 17, the drought had lowered the waters of the Tennessee drastically. It was as if the ancient Long Person had refused to cooperate in the removal of his people. This group of 1,070 walked 160 miles to Waterloo to board steamers, then traveled by wagon when the river again became too low. Only 722 reached Little Rock, where Smith put them on a light steamer for the rest of their trip.

At this point an appeal was sent to General Scott signed by Assistant Chief George Lowrey, Hair Conrad, Lewis Ross, Thomas Foreman, and Chief Going Snake. It read as follows:

"Spare their lives; expose them not to the killing effects of that strange climate, under the disadvantages of the present inauspicious season, without a house or shelter to cover them from above, or any kind of furniture to raise them from the bare ground, on which they may spread their blankets and lay their languid limbs, when fallen prostrate under the influence of disease."

The disastrous early removal parties convinced General Scott to suspend emigration until the fall. He then accepted a revolutionary proposal from Chief John Ross, with whom he had formed an earlier acquaintance in Washington. Scott, that great bear of a man, liked and respected the diminutive Principal Chief. "Let the Cherokee conduct their own removal," Ross urged him. "Give them the money to provision and supply themselves and hire their own conductors."

Although ex-President Andrew Jackson nearly had a fit of apoplexy about the U. S. military agreeing to such a proposal from "that scamp, Ross," John Ross was given full authority by General Scott. Unlike any other group of Indians, the Cherokee Nation would plan and conduct the final removal of their own people—the 12,000 Cherokees that remained in the camps.

Ross estimated the distance at 800 miles and the time required to go overland by wagon as 80 days. The contract agreed upon, revised upward to include the cost of soap, amounted to $65.88 per Indian. It would cover the cost of teams, wagons, rations, conductors, physicians, tolls, and other necessary purchases. Scott objected at first to the number of horses and wagons requested. He was confident, he wrote, that there were plenty of Cherokees "not only capable of marching twelve or fifteen miles a day, but to whom the exercise would be beneficial." Finally, though, General Scott accepted Ross's estimate.

"The case of the Cherokees," the Commissioner of Indian Affairs said, "is a striking example of the liberality of the Government in all its branches." But the money used for removal was not a gift. It was deducted from the payment of five million dollars (far less than the $20 million dollars the Cherokee Council estimated their remaining lands to be worth) promised the Cherokees in the Treaty of New Echota.

John Ross transferred the financial contract to his brother Lewis, a shrewd businessman, who would handle all the money involved with removal. Some in the anti-Ross party later said that the Rosses made

themselves wealthy by "selling their own people." However, a careful study of the records shows two things: the actual cost of removal left no room for any profit for the contractor, and John Ross was scrupulously honest—to the point of self-sacrifice. Not only did he never accept a penny from the removal monies, he even refused his salary as Chief during the time of the Trail of Tears.

Thirteen detachments led wholly by Cherokees and unaccompanied by Army escorts set out that fall toward the West, the Darkening Land associated with death in Cherokee traditions. The first party of 729 people, conducted by Hair Conrad, left on August 23. The last, numbering 231 Cherokees who were too old and weak to go earlier, departed on December 5. It was the only group to take the easier water route. John Ross was among the last to leave. He had stayed behind, making arrangements for each detachment as it set out.

The emigrants had been promised compensation for their seized property and livestock and the improvements on their lands, but the payments were often not forthcoming. The Reverend Jesse Bushyhead, who had loaded the beams from his church onto a wagon (to be re-erected near present-day Westville, Oklahoma, where it stands to this day), sent word back to John Ross from McMinnville, Tennessee, that his party had been forced to leave without their claims being satisfied and in fear of demands from fraudulent creditors.

As the Cherokees traveled northwest across Tennessee and Kentucky, through Nashville, Port Royal, Hopkinsville, and Princeton, they were cheated at toll roads and ferries. Evan Jones, one of the Baptist ministers traveling with the Cherokees, recorded in his journal around October 16 that they "paid forty dollars at the Walderns Ridge toll gate and the man agreed to let the other detachments pass at half price viz, 37½ (cents) for four-wheeled vehicles and 6½ for a horse. On the Cumberland mountains they fleeced us, 73 cents a wagon and 12½ cents a horse without the least abatement or thanks...."

Despite Scott's assertion that the walk would do them good, large numbers of Cherokees were ill when they set out on the trail. Burdened by a grief almost too deep to express, they grew sicker as their beloved mountains were lost from view. On October 24, after reaching Port Royal, Elijah Hicks noted that "the people are very loth to go on, and unusually slow in preparing for starting each morning. I am

OPPOSITE: A brilliant wildflower pokes through grasses in the Santa Fe National Forest on Glorieta Mesa at an elevation of about 6,000 feet. The spot is just south of the Navajos' Long Walk route.

not surprised at this, for they are moving not from choice to an unknown region not desired by them."

Hicks also recorded that Nocowee, one of the Cherokee leaders, had sunken into drunkeness, "given himself up to that bane of death and I have altogether lost his services. Our police has to drive him along the road sometimes fettered." White Path, a deeply venerated elder chief, was among those who died in the early stages of the trail. He was buried near Hopkinsville, Kentucky, a tall pole with a white flag marking his burial place for those who followed. White Path's memorial is one of the few Cherokee graves along the Trail of Tears that remains marked to this day.

Summer drought was followed by torrential rains and early snows. Many Cherokees were lightly clad for their journey, and short of blankets and winter coats—though Lewis Ross had provided as many as he could find in depots along the route. White citizens in more than one city along the way made donations to the distressed Cherokees.

By the time they reached the great rivers, the harsh winter had another unwelcome surprise in store for them. More than half the detachments were delayed as much as a month by ice floes at the crossings of the Ohio and the Missouri. James Mooney wrote that "over half a century hadn't sufficed to wipe out the memory of the miseries of that halt beside the frozen river, with hundreds of sick and dying penned up to keep out the January blast."

In two divisions, they at last crossed at Cape Girardeau and Green's Ferry and pushed on through Missouri, "the later detachments making a northerly course by Springfield," notes Mooney, "because those who had gone before had killed off all the game along the direct route...." It took no less than four months for any of the parties to reach their destination, much longer than Ross had estimated. The party led by Richard Taylor took the longest. On the road since September 20, they arrived at Fort Gibson on March 24, 1839. The journey along *Nunda ut sungi*, the Place Where We Cried, had ended.

Official records for the 13 parties list 447 deaths, 182 desertions, and 71 births. Among the recorded dead were the Reverend Jesse Bushyhead's sister—who died after finally crossing the Mississippi—and Quatie Ross, the wife of the Principal Chief—who succumbed to pneumonia soon after giving her only blanket to a freezing child. Far more fatalities went unrecorded. In the year from their imprisonment in the stockades to the last detachment's arrival in the West, at least a quarter of the Cherokees—4,000 souls—perished. Weakened by their terrible trial, still more died in the months after the Trail of Tears ended. Nearly all of the Cherokee elders and most of their young children could now be found only in the Darkening Land of the Dead.

For years after the end of the trail, Cherokee women of childbearing age found it impossible to conceive, their bodies too drained by the awful trials. Deceived, divided, burdened by grief, it seemed unlikely that a phoenix could ever rise again from the scattered ashes of what was once the great Cherokee Nation.

THE YEARS BEFORE THE NAVAJOS' LONG WALK

were marked by deep misunderstanding. Though described as fierce raiders and implacable warriors, first by the Spanish and then by American historians (who relied upon those earlier chroniclers as their sources), the Navajos, like the Cherokees, tried hard to make peace with the Americans.

European presence in the Southwest began in 1598 with Don Juan de Oñate, who brought 30 Spanish settlers into New Mexico. Soon, Pueblo people began to seek refuge among the Navajos to escape forced labor and enslavement by the Spanish. For the next 80 years, the Spanish ruled the Pueblos with an iron hand and sent expeditions into Dinetah for slaves. In return, the Navajos raided the Spanish settlements, stealing sheep and horses and taking captives.

By 1680, the Pueblos could bear it no longer. The great Pueblo Rebellion drove the Spanish out of New Mexico. Oral traditions of the Pueblo and Navajo people indicate that the practice of Navajo raiding either ended or was drastically diminished with the departure of the Spanish. In 1692, when the Spanish began to try to force their way back into New Mexico, the Navajos allied with the Pueblos to resist the white invaders. Despite resistance, the reconquest of New Mexico was completed by 1696.

The Navajos, however, were not defeated. For the next century and a half, a state of continual war existed between the Navajos and the New Mexican enemies, who continued to enslave them. Each time

The cracked mud of the Rio Puerco River southwest of Albuquerque still holds a subtle imprint of tracks left by human feet. It was here that Navajos on the Long Walk crossed the river as it coursed through a parched, barren landscape.

the Navajos signed a treaty, it was broken by New Mexican slave raiders, and the Navajos would retaliate.

In the meantime, the Navajos prospered. Their fields of corn and wheat filled the rich bottomlands along the rivers. In Canyon de Chelly, thousands of their peach trees bore sweet fruit. The herds of sheep, cattle, and goats increased in size. Navajo women adopted the craft of weaving with such success that their blankets became known as the best to be had. The ceremonials grew in number and intricacy as the Diné followed the ways given them by the Holy People.

Not all Navajos followed the ways of beauty. Some placed profit above spiritual balance and, in 1818, broke with their people. They began to serve as guides for New Mexican raids into Dinetah and even sold Navajo slaves themselves. Led by Antonio Sandoval, an ambitious and cunning man who came to leadership around 1830, they became known as the *Diné Ana'í*, the Enemy Navajos.

In 1845, the United States annexed Texas, and after fighting a one-sided war with Mexico, soon took possession of all of Mexico's northern provinces. Within them was Dinetah. On August 18, 1846, Gen. Stephen W. Kearney declared control over all citizens of the Territory of New Mexico, including Indian tribes. He felt certain that the Army could quickly end the warring between Navajos and New Mexicans by forcing the Navajos to obey the law. The fact that New Mexican trade in Navajo slaves was at the heart of the conflict was ignored.

The first mistake made by the Americans was the assumption that a Navajo chief could make a peace treaty binding all Navajos. Rather than a united tribal nation led by principal chiefs, the Navajos were many independent, isolated bands bound by ties of family and clan. While headmen had great responsibility for their own people, they could not tell other bands what to do. As a result, when treaties were signed, other Navajo bands considered themselves unaffected by someone else's agreements and continued to make raids. The United States made no such distinctions. If one Navajo committed a crime, all Navajos must be punished.

The second mistake was more subtle but no less disastrous. Seeking a Navajo envoy and an interpreter, the white soldiers chose Antonio Sandoval. Long accustomed to dealing with white men, he was, they thought, the perfect choice, but as the headman of the Cebolleta band of Navajos—the Diné Ana'í—other Navajos feared and mistrusted him. Sandoval was sent to parlay with all the Navajo headmen and tell them they must come to Santa Fe and pledge to end their warring. He returned after only ten days and led the Americans to understand that he had visited and spoken with all the Navajo headmen. (Even if he had used a helicopter, it would have been physically impossible for him to cover the vast territory of Dinetah and see dozens of leaders in such a short time.) The Navajo headmen, he told Jackson, had refused to come to meet with the "New Men"— the Americans. If the New Men wished to talk with the Navajos, they would have to go to them.

Communication between Navajos and Americans was complicated and confusing. At that time, no Americans could speak Navajo, nor were any Navajos fluent in English. The only language in common was Spanish—seldom spoken fluently by either side. Translation at peace parlays would be a three-step process. The Navajos would speak and then an interpreter—almost always Antonio Sandoval—would translate their words from Navajo into Spanish. An American who spoke Spanish would then translate the words from Spanish into English and repeat them to the American officer in charge.

On October 20, 1846, Capt. John Reid led an expedition into the heart of Navajo land to regain lost property and force the Navajos into peace negotiations. Narbona, an elderly and highly respected headman, met with Reid in a grassy valley near Red Lake. Narbona wanted peace. Though these New Men seemed much like their enemies, the New Mexicans, Narbona agreed to come in to Santa Fe to meet with them. Another expedition of 180 men led by Col. Alexander W. Doniphan, the military commander of New Mexico, marched into Dinetah close behind Captain Reid's party. At Ojo del Oso, they met

The Rio Puerco River weaves through the desert near Albuquerque, New Mexico. In long lines, Navajos struggled across the river bed with many miles to go.

FOLLOWING PAGES: A July thunderstorm brings the promise of rain near Merita, New Mexico. Farther to the east at Bosque Redondo, where captive Navajos were forced to relocate, such rain seldom fell.

Their beloved home now far behind, the Navajos would have traveled past Glorieta Mesa, now part of Santa Fe National Forest, at the left in this aerial view. To the right, I-25 runs along the route of the Long Walk, which converged with the Santa Fe Trail to skirt the mesa.

with a group of 500 Navajos led by 11 headmen, including a man named Long Earrings. Even filtered through two levels of translation, his logical answer to Colonel Doniphan is an accurate reflection of the way the Navajos viewed these new white men.

"Americans! You have a strange cause for war against the Navajos. We have waged war against the New Mexicans for many years. We have plundered their villages and killed many of their people.

You have lately commenced a war against the same people. You are powerful. You have great guns and many brave soldiers. You have therefore conquered them, the very same thing we have been attempting to do for so many years.

You now turn upon us for attempting what you have done yourselves. We cannot see why you have cause to quarrel with us for fighting the New Mexicans on the west, while you do the same on the east."

Doniphan replied that the New Mexicans were no longer enemies but friends under the protection of the U.S. Army. Strange as this concept of enemies becoming friends after a single campaign may have been to the long-suffering Navajos, Long Earrings and other Navajos present agreed there should be peace with the New Men. All 11 head-men signed the treaty calling for a lasting peace and the return of all prisoners. The treaty, which was not binding on all Navajos and made no mention of halting the slave trade that was the ultimate cause of all the troubles, was unworkable from the start.

Further treaties with the Navajos followed over the next 15 years. Expeditions sent to make war on them returned with little success. When American armies entered their lands, the Navajos would simply vanish, driving their herds with them, leaving only deserted fields and empty hogans that would then be burned by the soldiers. Or they would take refuge in such places as Canyon de Chelly. When an army entered the canyon, the Navajos climbed to the canyon rim or took shelter on top of the giant landform known as Fortress Rock at the junction of Canyon del Muerto and Black Rock Canyon.

The expedition of Col. J.M. Washington in August 1849 exemplified American high-handedness and gives another example of why the Navajos mistrusted the New Men. Washington's expedition included 123 New Mexican volunteers—virtually all of them slave traders who joined the expedition in the hope of profit. Several hundred Navajos, Narbona among them, met with Washington and James S. Calhoun, the new Indian agent.

It seemed as if things were going well. Then, as Sandoval was translating Calhoun's final remarks, a New Mexico volunteer turned his attention to a group of mounted Navajos. "That horse is one of mine that was stolen," he said. Without a moment's hesitation, Colonel Washington ordered his men to seize the horse. Charged by a group of armed, angry white men, the Navajos fled. Washington ordered his men to open fire, first with their rifles and then with a field gun. The artillery, one of the officers noted in his report, "threw in among them, very handsomely—much to their terror, when they were afar off and thought they could with safety relax their flight....These people evidently gave signs of being tricky and unreliable." Six Navajos died that day. Among them was Narbona. When he fell, one of the New Mexicans took his scalp.

Then, as if nothing had happened, Washington continued on to

Canyon de Chelly. Only a few nervous Navajos met with him there, none of them key leaders. Two minor headmen signed a treaty that, though ratified by the U.S. Senate, was worth less to the Navajos than the word of the Americans.

The Navajos continued to send delegations, year after year, to a succession of American governors in Santa Fe. They pointed out that they had returned many of their captives, many of whom would flee to their adopted Navajo families when they had the chance—yet few if any Navajos taken as slaves had been returned to their people. Though now prohibited, trade in Navajo slaves went unabated. The going price for a Navajo child was $200, too much profit to be resisted.

Again and again the Navajos explained they had no control over bands that had never signed a treaty. There were also outlaws among them—as among the white men—who followed no one's rules. No one seemed to listen. Some Navajo war leaders, such as Manuelito, gave up on the idea of peace with the Americans and their slave-trading allies.

In April 1860, an army of a thousand Navajos attacked Fort Defiance. Though only lightly garrisoned, the American soldiers beat them back.

By now, the Navajos faced another problem—hunger. The continued slave raids, the Army's destruction of Navajo food supplies, and a number of poor corn harvests had brought many Navajos close to starvation. A delegation of headmen led by Armijo, Delgadito, and Herrero convinced Col. Edward Canby of their sincerity, and a new treaty was signed in February 1861. Unlike some of his predecessors, Canby believed the Navajos were more sinned against than sinners. He hoped to protect them from the slave raiding he rightly saw as the main reason for their resistance. He began the practice of issuing food rations to the starving Navajos.

With the beginning of the American Civil War on April 13, 1861, one of the Confederate objectives was to seize New Mexico as a stepping-stone to the gold fields of California. U.S. troops were pulled from the forts in New Mexico and Arizona in response to the expected southern invasion from Texas. This withdrawal was disastrous for the Mescalero Apaches and the Navajos. The Navajos and Mescaleros had become dependent upon the forts for supplies and protection against their traditional enemies, the Comanches, the Utes, and the

New Mexican slave raiders. With the desertion of the forts, both Navajos and Mescaleros were forced to return to raiding as a means of survival. The fragile peace Canby had tried to forge in 1861 was ended.

The Civil War also brought a new military commander to New Mexico. In 1862, Gen. James H. Carleton led his "California Column" into New Mexico, replacing Canby. Because the Confederate threat had already ended with the defeat at Glorieta, the ambitious and overbearing general found himself with an army but no enemy in sight—except Indians. When the New Mexicans asked him to solve their Indian problems, Carleton was eager to oblige. His solution was to defeat them and then place them all on a reservation, following the well-established pattern of fort-building, military conquest, and removal. Colonel Canby had been in favor of a number of small, remote reservations within the traditional homeland of the Navajos. Carleton had another idea. He also had the one man better equipped than any other to wage a successful Indian war—Kit Carson.

Carson had gained fame first as a fur trader and hunter, then as a guide for John C. Frémont, helping him blaze trails to Oregon and California. Physically, Carson was not terribly imposing, but he knew the world of Native Americans as well as any white man of his time.

Adobe sentinels still at attention are all that remains of Officers' Row at Fort Union, near present-day Las Vegas, New Mexico. In its time the largest Army post in the Southwest, Fort Union was a resupply site for detachments of Navajos and their Army escorts on their way to Bosque Redondo. The ruins, now part of Fort Union National Monument, are the remains of the third fort in this spot, built in the 1860s and abandoned in 1891.

Though his new spouse, whom he was desperate to impress, was white, his previous wives had been Arapaho and Cheyenne.

As federal Indian agent for northern New Mexico, Carson had close ties with the Utes, ancient enemies of the Navajos. Yet it seems the Navajos liked him—despite his well-documented talent for killing Indians. Some called him "Red Clothes." To others he was "Rope-Thrower." Soon the Navajos would remember him only as one who turned his heart against them.

General Carleton issued orders for the Navajos to be removed to a distant reservation in eastern New Mexico. The place was called Bosque Redondo, and took its name from a round grove of cottonwood trees along the Pecos River. Carleton's new fort there was named Fort Sumner. It was a 400-mile walk from Fort Canby.

A board of officers inspected the Bosque Redondo site soon after Carleton chose it. It was, they said with some deference, a spot with good features. They did note that it wasn't perfect. Remote from any Army depot, it had a poor supply of timber, was prone to frequent flood, and lacked good water. They did not mention that the alkali soil was also ill-suited for agriculture, even with irrigation. As the future home of 9,000 Indians, the largest concentration of Native Americans anywhere on the continent, it was, in fact, absolutely wrong. But Car-

Their rough shelters scratched out of a harsh land, Navajos gather by their pitiful hogans at Fort Sumner, New Mexico, in 1866. Forced to build adobe houses for the Army, the Navajos' own homes were made out of whatever was available in the stark, treeless landscape. The first hogans at Bosque Redondo were little more than holes dug in the dry earth and covered by sticks and brush.

Company quarters at Fort Sumner, New Mexico, provide sharp contrast to the housing of the captive Navajos. The adobe structures, built by forced labor of the Navajos, were exclusively for the use of the white soldiers.

leton saw the model reservation he would create, an oasis in the desert where savages would be converted into model civilized farmers. It would be his "Fair Carletonia."

General Carleton's deadline of July 20, 1863 came and went with few Navajos coming into Fort Canby. The only ones who peacefully surrendered—and they were immediately sent off to Bosque Redondo—were the old slave-trading allies of the Army, the Diné Ana'í. On September 19, 1863, a group of 51 Navajos, 43 of whom were Diné Ana'í, were the first to reach their place of exile at the end of the Long Walk.

But they were not the first Indians to reach the Bosque. As a first step in subduing the "hostiles" of New Mexico, Col. Kit Carson and his army had been engaged in a campaign against the Mescalero Apaches to drive them to, as Carleton put it, their "brutal senses." Carson's troops killed the Apaches when they were cornered, took prisoners when they could, and burned every Indian cornfield and home they could find on the theory that if their families were starving, the Mescaleros would lose their will to fight.

By February 1863 all of the Mescaleros had been killed, taken as prisoners, or had fled to Mexico and the White Mountains of Arizona. Three hundred and fifty Mescaleros arrived at Bosque Redondo before the Navajos. Carleton assumed the two tribes would get along well together, being closely related, but this was yet another of his miscalculations. The Navajos and Mescaleros were old enemies.

The winter of 1863 was made bitter not only by the unusual cold,

Ready to strike if necessary, a rattlesnake coils near Fort Union National Monument. Feared by the whites, the rattlesnake is respected by native peoples for its courage in always warning an enemy before attacking. Seen as sacred among the native peoples of the Southwest, its presence is associated with the coming of rain.

but by the taste of fear. Carson's campaign against the Navajos was like that against the Apaches, but on a much larger scale. The period the Navajos now call *Nidahonidzóódą́ą́'*, the "Time of Being Herded Around," had begun.

Carson's tactics were absolutely ruthless. Anyone who came within rifle range was shot down. Fields of corn, beans, and squash were destroyed, wells and waterholes were filled in or contaminated, and hogans burned. Navajo animals—their horses, sheep, cattle, and goats—were killed or driven off. Canyon de Chelly no longer provided safety, although some oral traditions tell of one group of 300 Navajos who avoided capture throughout the Carson campaign by seeking refuge on the top of *Tse'lá*, Fortress Rock, in Canyon de Chelly.

Carson's troops entered Canyon de Chelly on January 11th and 12th. By January 14, starving Navajos began to come out of the canyon and surrender to Carson, who directed them to Fort Canby to await removal. Throughout that year and the next the

Marking a road that still seems to run through the middle of nowhere, deep ruts lead out of Fort Union National Monument toward the distant mountains. The road was used by the fort to gather wood and hunt deer in the mountains. This barren landscape presented itself in every direction to the eyes of the Navajos who were held at Bosque Redondo.

scorched-earth policy continued. All the Navajos owned was destroyed: their crops, their homes, their livestock. Even the peach orchards were cut down.

On February 1, the first hungry Navajos arrived at the forts. Within a week, there were over 800. The trickle became a flood as more and more Navajos surrendered and came in to Fort Canby and Fort Wingate, where they were held awaiting transfer to Bosque Redondo.

Some 2,000 Navajos never surrendered, seeking refuge in the broken lands around Navajo Mountain and Black Mountain. So many Navajos were now at the forts that they strained the Army's resources. There were few blankets and food was scant. The U.S. Army gave out rations of white flour to the Indians with no instructions on how to use it. The Navajos either tried to eat it raw or boiled it in water to make thin soup. It made them sick. Within two weeks, 126 Navajos died at Fort Canby from dysentery and exposure.

Some 2,000 Navajos began the 400-mile walk from Fort Canby to Fort Sumner on March 4. Unlike the Cherokees, who conducted their own people on the Trail of Tears, the Navajos on the Long Walk were driven like sheep by the Army. People unable to walk because they were doubled up with cramps from the strange food in their bellies were left behind or shot. Sometimes children too small to walk

Photographs taken at Bosque
Redondo in 1866 convey images
of sad exile. A soldier stands
guard over Navajos (above) who
may have been brought together
for rations, for work detail, or
for a head count to see how many
had escaped. A young Navajo
man (opposite, left) holds himself
like a warrior before the camera.
A Navajo woman (opposite, right)
carries her baby in a cradleboard.
Navajo women (left) lean together
as if to support each other in
their suffering.

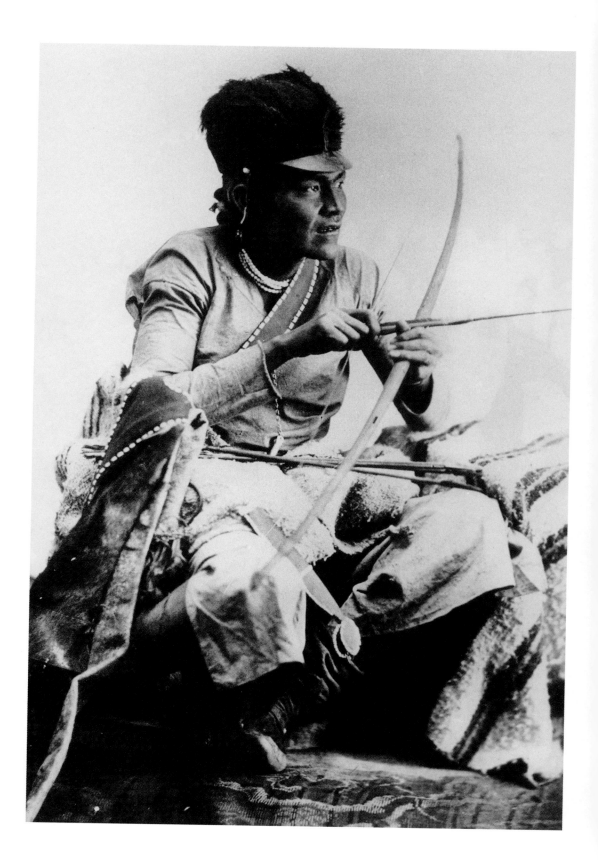

were carried on ox-drawn wagons, and those who could not keep up were allowed to ride on a horse or a wagon. More often, though, theirs was a different fate.

Howard Gorman, a former member of the Navajo Tribal Council born in 1900, recalled descriptions of the Long Walk passed down in oral tradition. "On the journey," he said, "the Navajos went through all kinds of hardships, like tiredness and having injuries. And when those things happened, the people would hear gun shots in the rear. But they couldn't do anything about it. They just felt sorry for the ones being shot. Sometimes they would plead with the soldiers to let them go back and do something, but they were refused. This is how the story was told by my ancestors."

OPPOSITE: A Navajo man at Bosque Redondo poses with a bow and arrow. At times he would have had to defend himself against Comanches and New Mexicans, who frequently raided "Fair Carletonia."

From Fort Canby the trail led to Fort Wingate and then across the Rio Grande to Peralta, where the people turned north to Albuquerque. As they continued to move east, *Tsoodził,* (Mount Taylor), the last of their sacred mountains, was lost to their view. The people wept when they could no longer see it. Some of the old people perished, the pain of leaving Dinetah too great for their hearts to bear.

The straggling lines of people were sometimes four or five miles long. Before the numbers of Indians being moved became too great, each column of Navajos was forced to detour north to be paraded through the streets of Santa Fe, visible evidence of the utter defeat of a once proud nation. The journey lasted close to three weeks.

Many Navajo children were stolen away and sold as they were brought in or taken captive by raiders who swept down on the lines of march. As many as one in ten of the Navajo people ended up as slaves during that terrible time.

By the end of February, Carleton realized he had underestimated the situation. He had assumed the Navajo nation numbered only 5,000 people. More than 8,000 eventually arrived at Fort Sumner. Carleton directed Maj. Henry Wallen, commander at the fort, "to make timely estimates for the bread and salt required for all these Indians, and to have a margin of food on hand for at least fifty days. There must be no mistake about having enough for them to eat, if we have to kill horses and mules for them." Soon, however, the food began to run out. Everyone, including the soldiers, was put on half rations.

And still the flow of Navajos continued, as did the suffering. In mid-April, 2,400 Navajos began the Long Walk. Like all of those who had been driven along the trail before them, they were poorly clad and weak from hunger. Heavy snow began to fall and sharp winds cut across the flat, open land. The quartermaster wagons were soon filled with Indians too weak to walk. The rest stumbled on as best they could, hands and feet numb with frostbite. No one knows how many died on the journey, but the frozen corpses of Navajos marked their passage along much of the way.

Things did not improve when the Navajos reached Bosque Redondo. They called the place *Hwééldi,* Place of the Wind. It is a name every Navajo still knows in the way Christians know the name of Purgatory. The only firewood to be found was mesquite, and even that was so scarce that people had to walk four or five miles to gather enough for cooking. The water was salty and bitter and there was never enough food.

Still, Carleton pressed on with his great "civilizing" experiment. The Navajos were set to work building adobe houses for the troops. Their own shelters were rough hogans, usually holes dug in the ground and covered as well as possible with brush and earth. They were ordered to plow the fields and plant corn as the white men did, but the crops failed. At times the people were so desperate for food that they would search through the manure of the soldiers' horses for corn.

One February more than 100 Navajos froze to death when they were refused permission to stop plowing the infertile fields, even though a storm was sweeping in. On the last day of each month, everyone was counted, to make sure no one had slipped away. Even though they were closely watched, the Navajos were still prey to raids from the Comanches, who would frequently come onto the reservation and run off what little stock the Navajos had. After two years in captivity, the Mescalero Apaches managed to escape from Bosque Redondo, leaving only the Navajos. Through it all, like a politician practicing spin control, Carleton kept insisting that all was well.

In time, the dismal failure of Carleton's great plan was obvious, and the plight of the Navajos no longer hidden. Fair Carletonia was a concentration camp. Carleton was removed from his post in 1868, and a peace commission was sent to Bosque Redondo to make a new treaty. There was some talk of sending the Navajos to Oklahoma, even though the 7,500 Navajos who remained at the Bosque in 1868 would have been more of a burden than the Oklahoma Indian Territory would wish to bear. At any rate, the Navajos refused.

Some newspapers of the time editorialized that the Indians should have been pushed farther west and never brought toward the east. A congressional committee headed by Senator James Doolittle of Wisconsin concluded that the underlying cause of the conflict could be found in the generations of slave raids conducted against the Navajos. The Doolittle Commission found that the Navajos at Bosque Redondo were starving, their herds were gone, and they had no wood for fuel. They agreed that a terrible human injustice was being done, and eventually signed a treaty that would allow the Navajos to return to a reservation in their homeland.

The Navajos tell another story of their return. A headman named Barboncito had advised his people at Hwééldi, but his words and ceremonies were not heeded. One day he conducted a ceremony in which the people formed a big circle and closed in until a coyote was trapped inside. According to Mose Denejolie, whose grandfather told him the story, Barboncito caught the coyote and put a piece of white shell in its mouth. When the coyote was released, she turned clockwise and walked off to the west. Barboncito said, "There it is, we'll be set free."

Barboncito represented the Navajos during the treaty negotiations, during which he faced Gen. William Tecumseh Sherman. "I am speaking to you now as if I was speaking to a spirit," he said, "and I wish you to tell me when you are going to take us to our own country....I hope to God you will not ask me to go to any other country except my own."

Miraculously, Barboncito's words were heeded. Nine other spokesmen selected by the tribe echoed his words. On June 1, 1868, 28 Navajo headmen representing their people, Barboncito among them, pressed their thumbs to the final document. The 29th man, Delgadito, the brother of Barboncito, was the only one able to sign his name.

Eventually the Navajos were allowed to return to a small reservation in their own homeland. They were provided livestock and goods that would at least partially replace what they had lost. Another Long Walk took place, but this one brought an entire nation back to its true home—the sacred mountains of Dinetah.

FOLLOWING PAGES:
The Long Walk and the return journey from Bosque Redondo both crossed the Pecos River southeast of the town of Dilia, New Mexico. One of the few dependable sources of water in the region, the Pecos was incorporated into both routes.

ENDURING WAYS

These mountains and the land between them
Are the only things that keep us strong.
From them, and because of them we prosper.
It is because of them that we eat plants
        and good meat.

We carry soil from the Sacred Mountains in a
        prayer bundle that we call dah nidíilyééh.
Because of this bundle we gain sheep, horses,
        and cattle.
We gain possessions and thing of value,
        turquoise, necklaces and bracelets.
With this we speak, with this we pray.
This is where the prayers begin.

from the poem "Sacred Mountains"
by George Blueeyes

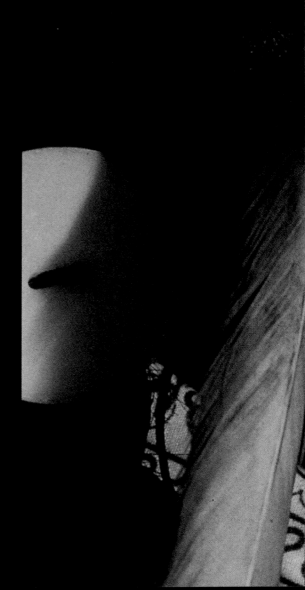

But here the hills are quietly breathing
        the earth is a warm glowing blanket
        holding me in her arms
            It is here among the sunset in
                    every plant
                    every rock
                    every shadow
                    every movement
                    every thing
        I relive visions of ancient stories
            First Woman and First Man
            their children stretched across
                    these eternal sandstones

            a deep breath
            she brings me sustenance
            life
        and I will live to tell my children these things.

from the poem "At Mexican Springs"
by Laura Tohe (Navajo)

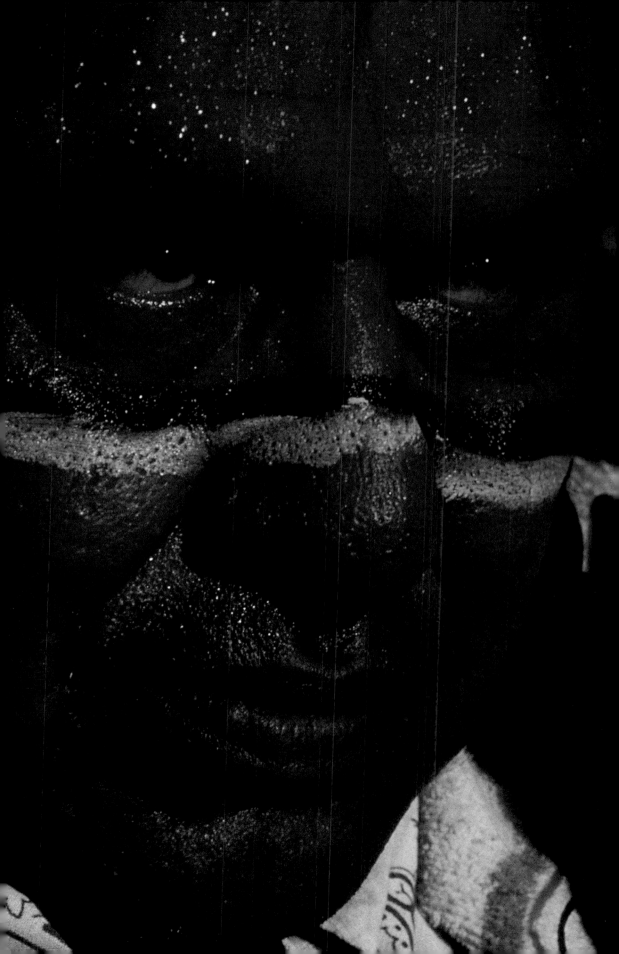

DRIVING THROUGH THE VALLEY OF THE

Oconaluftee in Cherokee, North Carolina, J.T. Garrett, a county health director and member of the Eastern Band of Cherokees, told me a story of his son, Michael, who met a young Navajo man in college. A conversation between the two students turned to history, and went something like this:

"Remember how our people were forced to leave their land?" Michael asked.

"Oh yes," said the Navajo man. "Our people cried when they could no longer see our sacred mountains."

"Remember how the United States government broke its promises to our people?"

"Yes, in every treaty that we signed," the Navajo agreed.

"Remember how many of our people we lost while we were being held in captivity?"

"Yes," said the Navajo. "Most of our elders and little children died."

"But even so, despite it all, our people found strength in our old ways and we survived."

"That is certainly true," said the Navajo.

"And that white man—whose name I don't want to say—even though our people had helped him in the past, when he came to power, he betrayed us."

"That is true," said the Navajo man. "Kit Carson treated us badly."

OPPOSITE: In the Cherokee Masked Dance, or Booger Dance, dangerous outsiders are defined and reduced to caricatures.

PAGES 160-161: The ancient buttes of Monument Valley rise through a shroud of mist.

PRECEDING PAGES: His eyes holding visions of the past, ceremonial dancer Ron Moses wears paint and feathers adapted from the dress of the Plains tribes at the Cherokee National Holiday Powwow in Tahlequah, Oklahoma.

"No, I was talking about Andrew Jackson," Michael replied.

It was only then that they realized that each of them had been talking about the history of their own people, and not the other's.

The trials of the Cherokee and Navajo Nations did not end with the Trail of Tears or with the Long Walk. The Cherokee Nation found division and civil strife in their new lands. Then came the devastation of the American Civil War, in which the Cherokee Nation was as divided as the American North and South, sometimes fighting brother against brother. Yet another rebuilding of the Cherokee Nation was followed by federal confiscation of Cherokee holdings and the near termination of their government.

The Navajos were faced with the daunting task of recovering from the trauma of years in captivity. They returned to a much diminished homeland surrounded by former enemies. At the start of the 20th century, the survival of both nations seemed tenuous at best.

Yet in time, both the Cherokees and the Navajos managed to thrive. They faced unexpected turns and roadblocks placed before them by ill-considered federal policies that often proved devastating to the very people they were supposed to benefit. But the paths taken by these Native Americans were lit by the ancient fires of their traditions and shaped by their remarkable ability to adapt as they sought balance between two worlds.

CHEROKEE EMIGRANTS FOUND THAT THE old settler Cherokees were not eager to be ruled by the new majority just arrived from the Southeast. The "Treaty Party" led by the Ridges, Elias Boudinot, and his brother Stand Watie, also opposed the greater body of Cherokees loyal to John Ross.

The bitter memories of the Trail of Tears and the death sentences against those who had signed away Cherokee land lay like embers waiting to burst into flame. For a short time there was an uneasy truce. Then, on June 22, 1839, near the new Cherokee capital of Tahlequah, Major Ridge, his son John Ridge, and Elias Boudinot were killed by assassins. Stand Watie escaped. To the later sorrow of his enemies, he would never forget that bloody day.

Though it seems John Ross had no part in those killings and tried

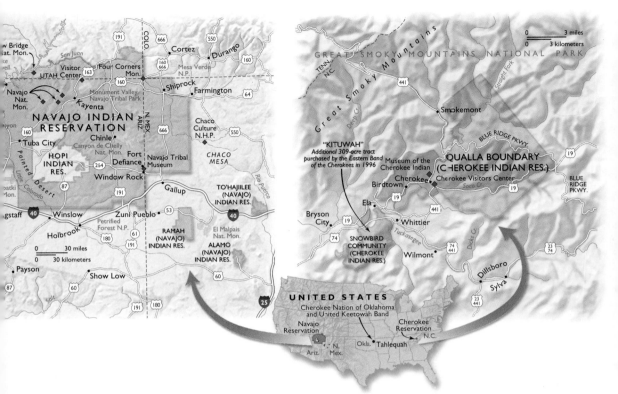

to prevent them, people in Ross's party sanctioned the executions. Other deaths on both sides followed until peace was finally restored. One of the principal architects of that peace was Sequoyah, whose prestige was great among all the quarreling factions. A government uniting all the Cherokees in the new Indian lands was formed. John Ross was again elected as Principal Chief of the Cherokee Nation.

For 15 years the Cherokees enjoyed a "golden age," rebuilding their schools and farms, churches, stores, and government buildings. Then the Cherokee Nation was torn apart with the American Civil War. Though John Ross, supported by the Keetoowahs, a largely full-blood Cherokee Society deeply opposed to slavery, urged neutrality, slave-owning Cherokees pushed through a treaty with the South. Led by Stand Watie, who became a Confederate general—the last Confederate general to surrender—two Cherokee regiments were formed for service with the Confederacy. Eventually, many Cherokees, including John Ross, declared for the Union.

The Civil War was disastrous for the Cherokee people. Many Cherokees were killed on both sides—including two of John Ross's sons—and their new homeland was devastated. Gen. Stand Watie and

Movie star and hometown son, Wes Studi takes on the role of Grand Marshall in the 47th annual Cherokee National Holiday parade in Tahlequah, Oklahoma. Studi played a tough Pawnee in the film Dances With Wolves, Magua *in* The Last of the Mohicans, *and the lead role in* Geronimo. *Walking behind him are Principal Chief Chad Smith of the Cherokee Nation (right), a direct descendant of Redbird Smith, and Deputy Principal Chief Hastings Shade (left), a direct descendant of Sequoyah.*

Young men play stick ball, a game related to lacrosse, during the annual Cherokee Fall Festival in Cherokee, North Carolina. The traditional game instills important values such as inclusion and cooperation, and reaffirms much of what it means to be Cherokee.

his armies scoured the countryside, evening old scores. They burned Tahlequah to the ground, destroying nearly every Cherokee home and farm, school, church, and civil building.

By the end of the Civil War, a third of the 21,000 Cherokees had perished, but the spirit of the people endured. When the U.S. government presented them with the Cherokee Reconstruction Treaty of 1866, which would have divided the Western Cherokees into two separate nations, Principal Chief John Ross went to Washington one more time to fight for Cherokee unity. On April 3, 1866, Dennis N. Cooley, the Commissioner of Indian Affairs, visited the old chief's room in Jay's Hotel. John Ross's body was weak, but his spirit was unbroken.

Commissioner Cooley leaned over the dignified old man who lay there on his bed. "I learn, Mr. Ross," Cooley said, "that you are 75 years of age and have served your nation over 50."

"Yes Sir," John Ross whispered in reply. "I am an old man and have served my people and the government of the United States a long time, over 50 years. My people have kept me in the harness, not of my seeking, but of their own choice. I have never deceived them, and now I look back, not one act of my public life rises up to upbraid me. I have done the best I could, and today, upon this bed of sickness,

As evening falls, Cherokee elder Walker Calhoun builds a fire in preparation for a stomp dance, which will probably last through the night. Walker Calhoun revived this traditional dance among the Eastern Cherokees, having gone to Oklahoma years ago to get coals from the sacred fire to bring the ancient flame back to his people.

my heart approves all I have done. And still I am John Ross, the same John Ross of former years, unchanged."

Those were John Ross's last public words. He died on August 1, 1866 after winning a final battle for his people. The treaty signed that same day recognized a single Cherokee Nation.

That nation was challenged in a dramatic way when the Congressional Act of March 3, 1893 empowered the Dawes Commission to put a new Indian policy called allotment into effect. The United States had decided that Indians could never enjoy the full benefits of civilization while they followed their old ways. Communal use of the land and tribally chosen governments were seen as backward. Under allotment, all Indians would be listed in tribal rolls. Tribal governments would be dissolved, and former Indian lands would be divided, giving each Indian 160 acres. Whatever land was left over would be lost to them.

Not surprisingly, the 41,000 Cherokees of Indian Territory voted overwhelmingly against this. Enrollment was forced upon them. The Cherokee government was ordered to be dissolved by March 1906—though it continued in restricted form until June 1914. The "final" Principal Chief, William C. Rogers, was allowed to remain in his office until 1917 to sign the deeds needed for the transfer of Cherokee lands.

Many Cherokees refused to be enrolled, especially the Keetoowahs. They sought refuge in the hills, and when captured, chose to go to jail rather than enroll. At the same time, dishonest whites seeking Indian land showed up at enrollment centers, pretending to be mixed-blood Indians. It is estimated that there were about 100,000 Native Americans eligible for enrollment, counting all the tribes in the Indian Territory. Over 300,000 people attempted to enroll.

The Cherokees still hoped a separate Indian state would be formed out of their land. Many wanted it to be named Sequoyah, after the great Cherokee peacemaker. Instead, when statehood came on November 16, 1907, a single state named Oklahoma was created. On that same day a mock wedding was performed in the new Oklahoma capital of Guthrie between a couple portraying "Miss Indian Territory" and "Mr. Oklahoma Territory."

Statehood and allotment also began what some Cherokees refer to as a second Trail of Tears. "Dawes said in 1881 that there was not a pauper in the entire Cherokee Nation, and that the Cherokee Nation owed not a dollar," Principal Chief Chad Smith explained to me, "The fault of our system was apparent—there was no selfishness, which is at the bottom of civilization. We were on a land surplus/subsistence economy. When the land was allotted, it was a deliberate attempt to change the economy to a landlord/renter cash economy.

"In 1907 we had 7.5 million acres," he continued. "By 1920 we had lost 90 percent of our land. By 1930 we were solely dependent upon a cash economy and we were disenfranchised. Then the Depression hit. Half the population of the Cherokee Nation in Oklahoma left during the Depression because of the economy. The first Trail of Tears was political coercion. The second Trail of Tears was the result of very hostile federal policies. The allotment policy was far more devastating to us than the removal policy."

FOR A TIME, THE ONLY CHEROKEE NATION

recognized by the United States was the much smaller community of Cherokees who had managed to remain in North Carolina. More than a thousand Cherokees had found refuge in their old homeland in the deep coves and on the mountain slopes of North Carolina. (Another group of Cherokees formed a loose confederacy of refugee Indians in the early 1800s in Texas. Many from that Texas band, along with Kickapoos and Delawares, eventually settled in Mexico near Guadalajara, where their descendants live to this day.)

North Carolina took a different approach to its native peoples from that of the other southern states. Article 12 of the Treaty of New Echota, as amended, stated that Cherokees averse to removal could become citizens and remain in the state of North Carolina. About 1,200 Cherokees did just that. Other Cherokees who escaped from removal made their way to North Carolina and found refuge among the "citizen Cherokees." Today the large Native American population of North Carolina includes not only Cherokees but also Catawbas, Lumbees, and Haliwa-Saponi.

The status of the Eastern Cherokees in the early 1800s remained uncertain. Though legally severed from the main body of removed Indians, their lands in North Carolina had been divested by the treaty. In the struggles to keep their land, one of their greatest allies was William H.

Thomas, a white man who had lost his parents at an early age. In 1817, at the age of 12, he was adopted by Chief Yonaguska of the Oconaluftee Cherokees. Before long, the orphaned white boy learned to speak and write Cherokee. He would never waver in his lifelong devotion to his adopted people.

By the time of the Cherokee removal, William Thomas was a successful businessman. He helped the Eastern Cherokees led by Chief Yonaguska purchase land which they held in North Carolina as "citizen Indians," and lobbied in Washington and North Carolina that the Removal Act would not affect them. Eventually, there was an informal recognition of their right to remain.

Thomas supported the Confederacy during the Civil War. He formed the Thomas Legion, including over 200 Cherokee volunteers in their own companies. These Cherokee companies, famed for their unparalleled woodcraft—were used to hunt down deserters, enemy scouts, and Union sympathizers in the mountains. Their loyal service did not go unnoticed. In 1866, the North Carolina legislature granted the Oconaluftee Citizen Cherokees permission to remain permanently on the Qualla Boundary in the western part of the state. In 1868, they wrote their own constitution, elected a chief and council, and were recognized as a separate Indian tribe by the federal government.

While the Oklahoma Cherokees were stripped of self-governance, the more isolated North Carolina Cherokees managed to avoid allotment and overcome an 1886 Supreme Court ruling that they were no longer a tribe. Under the leadership of Chief Nimrod Jarrett Smith, they applied for and received a corporate charter.

One of Smith's visits to Washington attracted the attention of pioneering ethnologist James Mooney. Mooney traveled to North Carolina, where his respectful approach gained the trust of prominent Cherokee elders. Mooney spent more than a decade visiting the Qualla Boundary to record the traditional stories, knowledge, and sacred formulas of Eastern Cherokee elders, in particular Ayuh ini, from whom most of Mooney's material came. Much of the western world's contemporary knowledge about Cherokee traditions and culture comes from Mooney's landmark volumes *The Sacred Formulas of the Cherokees* (1891) and *Myths of the Cherokee* (1900).

Will West Long, an apprentice to Ayuh ini who served as Mooney's

Covered in mud, these boys recall the legend of the Mud People who rose from the earth to become the Cherokees. Riding in the back of a pickup truck in the 47th annual Cherokee National Holiday parade in Tahlequah, Oklahoma, they remind the Cherokee people who watch to always remember the land from which they came.

scribe, was deeply inspired by the project. Long went on to attend Hampton Institute in Virginia before returning in 1904 to the Qualla Boundary where, for the rest of his life, he was a major force in maintaining Cherokee traditions. Today the Eastern Cherokee Band, still a separate nation from their western relatives, numbers about 9,000.

In April 1984, the two Cherokee nations came together for a historic joint council, the first since the Trail of Tears. The two Principal Chiefs, Ross Swimmer and Robert Youngdeer, presided as 20,000 people gathered in a remote mountain meadow at Red Clay, the old Cherokee meeting grounds in Georgia. As the crowd watched in silence, two young runners carried torches to the chiefs for a ceremonial lighting. They had run 130 miles from Qualla Boundary, North Carolina, carrying a spark from the sacred fire that had burned for centuries.

AT THE CHEROKEE TRIBAL COMPLEX IN Tahlequah, Oklahoma, after more than six decades of dormancy, the Cherokee Nation held elections for a Principal Chief in 1970. Five years later, the Cherokee Nation enacted a new constitution. Though there was no real land base, no reservation, the Cherokee Nation gained strength through tribally run businesses and through its government programs and services. Though nearly disbanded as a people in the early 20th century, a strong Cherokee identity had remained among the Principal People. Cherokees began registering in the revitalized nation. By 1987, there were 72,000 members, and tribal assets had grown to more than $40 million. By the end of the 20th century, the Cherokee Nation had the largest number of members (308,000) of any tribe in the United States.

Recently elected Chief Chad "Corntassel" Smith is a great grandson of Senator Redbird Smith, who resisted federal policies at the end of the 19th century and refused to accept his allotment. A former tribal prosecutor and a strong proponent of Cherokee language, arts, and culture, Chief Smith also gained a reputation as a maker of clocks that tell time using Cherokee syllabary before he entered into tribal politics. His clocks hang in a number of the offices in the tribal complex.

Principal Chief Chad Smith says he'd like to follow in the footsteps of Redbird Smith, who served in the Cherokee Nation Senate in the late 1800s and reestablished the traditional religion. When he refused his allotment, the government arrested him and threw him into jail. He fought to preserve the Cherokee government and the right to hold a communal land title. "To us, he's a patriot," Principal Chief Smith told me.

"I'd like to follow in the footsteps of my grandmother, who went from home to home in the 1930s and 40s getting nickels and dimes trying to send a lawyer to Washington to try to preserve or revitalize the Cherokee Nation as a government," he said, "Or to follow in the footsteps of my father, who was a good Cherokee man and provided for us and tried to allow us to survive one more generation after World War II, after the efforts of the boarding schools to try to eradicate our culture and our language and after the Bureau of Indian Affairs policies to assimilate us."

Deputy Chief Hastings Shade has been honored by his nation as a living treasure for his efforts to share and preserve the traditions of his people. His book, *Myths, Legends and Old Sayings,* published in 1994, reveals some of the depth of his awareness. Being with him is like visiting a living library of Cherokee folk culture.

When I asked about his impressive knowledge of the Cherokee traditions and how he came by it, he explained, "There's no secret to it, just listen to the elders. When they look at you, they see you—not just *who* you are but *what* you are just by lookin' at you. Once they realize you are there for the sake of the Cherokee people, they begin to open up and tell you the old ways. I listen to the elders and I try not to abuse the faith they have in me, but use it to teach."

The Cherokees have survived because of their ability to adapt and live in a different culture, he explained. "When the Creator created man he also created things. He created the books, the weapons, the tools, and the cooking utensils. He said he would give the Indian the books, the white-skinned people the weapons, the black-skinned people the tools, and the yellow-skinned people the cooking utensils. We looked at these books and saw that we could not use them to go out and hunt with. So in our infinite wisdom, we switched. We got the weapons and the white-skinned people got the books.

"Our elders say we've paid for doing that over the years," he continued. "Now we have to get the book back. We're learning. We have our own lawyers who are looking at the treaties and how they were written. Our young people are getting better educated, learning the jobs of this age."

Hastings Shade believes that the Cherokee language is vital to maintain Cherokee culture. "The language is important because of fire," he told me. "They say that fire only understands Cherokee. To keep it going we always have to have that language. Everybody knows that language changes—it may be broken later on, we may have lost some of the little sounds that make the words as we know them, it may be spoken haltingly, but the fire will still understand.

"According to legends," he said, "we were the first Indian people to have the fire. It's a gift from the Creator. When Europeans came and saw us dancing around the fire, they thought we were worshiping Satan. They associate fire with hell and eternal suffering. But we see fire as a gift from the Creator, a gift to use."

Later I visited with Evelyn Conley, who, like many Cherokee women, fills a number of roles. She is assistant to the deputy chief, a major force in developing a Cherokee crafts organization, and a deeply influential advisor on Cherokee language and culture for her husband, writer Robert Conley. Evelyn is a living reminder of the central place Cherokee women have always held.

"In the community I come from, the women were very strong," she told me, "but they were very silent about some of the work they did. When you look at the survival of the matrilineal clan system, you have to know that there are strong women holding these families together. Throughout our history, the women were always there to support the family, hold it together, and preserve the things that bind us.

"Maybe we don't do ceremonies the way they did a hundred years ago," said Evelyn, "but some of that survives in us in the way we do things today. You can look at the blending of the old ways with the new as a good way to get around the dominant culture saying you have to be Christian and this is the way you have to do things.

"The way to survive is to accept things and blend them together," she continued. "Some might say that this creates a kind of schizophrenic style, but I think that's how so many of our ways have survived. We preserved the language by singing hymns in Cherokee. The Cherokee Going to Water ceremony was blended with the Baptismal ceremony. A lot of people get mad when they think of Christianity and what it has done to the people. But I think the preservation of our language was best done when they translated the Bible into Cherokee and taught everybody to read the syllabary."

Even so, in Cherokee, North Carolina, most of those who can speak Cherokee are over age 50. That makes Tom Belt, age 46, one of the youngest speakers. Until recently, he taught the language in grades three through six, one hour a week, a job to which he may one day return. He now works as a counselor in a Bureau of Indian Affairs funded program for troubled Cherokee youth.

"We need total immersion," he told me. "When we lose our language, we lose our culture. When you speak in Cherokee, you see the world in a different way. In English, everything centers around the individual. Everything starts with I. If you see something, in English you say, 'I see a bear.' In Cherokee you say 'Yona jigotiha. The bear I see it.' That draws attention to the bear first, and it shows respect to the person you are talking to by drawing their attention to it and allowing them to perceive it before you put yourself in between."

Tom took me to the field where a mound called Kituwah rises

gently, encircled by nearby hills. For thousands of years this place served as the ceremonial center for the Cherokees, and was the home for the sacred fire. The importance of the area had been long forgotten by most people, but recently the Cherokees bought back the mound and 300 surrounding acres.

We walked around the mound counterclockwise and entered the circle from the east. "Every year" explained Tom, "the people in all of the villages would each take a turtle shell and fill it with earth from the floor of their house. Then each village would gather all of that earth together into a big basket and they would carry it here to this place and spread the earth out here."

Tom took two cigarettes, broke off the filters, and handed me one. I stripped the paper from it, and after Tom made his offering, I sprinkled it over the place where the fire once burned—and will burn again.

"There are fifty chiefs buried here in a circle around the center, holding hands to protect the fire. Last spring, when I told my students about how the mound was built, a fifth grade girl said, 'Why can't we do that?' It wasn't a question; it was something we needed to do. When a child says something like that, you have to do it. Once the idea started, it couldn't be stopped. The children brought earth from their homes in plastic bags. We found seven turtle shells, and seven men on the mound spread the earth out as the children brought it up. It was the first time in over 160 years."

To the west, where a field of tall corn would soon be harvested by the school children and shared in a feast, a red-tailed hawk circled higher and higher, its tail a fan of sunlight.

FAR BELOW ME, A NAVAJO MAN WITH TWO border collies herded his sheep past an ancient Anasazi cliff dwelling in Canyon de Chelly. Visitors from all over the world drive along the rim of the canyon. Some explore parts of this great natural labyrinth with Navajo tour guides, but only Navajos are allowed to live within the canyon's sacred depths. Watching that herd of sheep flow gently across the canyon floor, where peach trees bloom again 140 years after Kit Carson's troops destroyed the Navajo orchards, I thought of how the people reclaimed their homeland.

The Navajos, reduced to "a band of paupers" as they returned to their homeland from Hwééldi, were described by John Pyle, their Indian agent, only a decade later as "a nation of prosperous, industrious, shrewd…intelligent people." How did this happen?

There are two ways to answer that question. The first uses the logic of a European mind. The second comes from perceiving the world through the eyes of Native Americans. It is appropriate that there is more than one way of seeing, for like the contemporary Navajos and Cherokees, who have learned to live in balance in two worlds, we may find truth in both explanations.

The Diné answer is as brief as it is moving. Because we were able to return to our sacred land, the Navajos say, the land took care of us.

Yet the original reservation set aside for the Navajos in 1868 amounted to less than one quarter of the present-day reservation. A number of factors over the next 50 years made the land held by Navajos greatly increase at a time when other native nations were losing more of theirs. First of all, it was fortunate for the Navajos that General Carleton's expectations of rich mines of gold and silver in Dinetah did not turn out to be true. Otherwise, the return home as well as

Lorraine Drywater cradles buffalo-grass dolls she made at her home near Tahlequah, Oklahoma. To her, each doll is special and has a personality all its own. Her grandmother made such dolls for children in the hard times after removal.

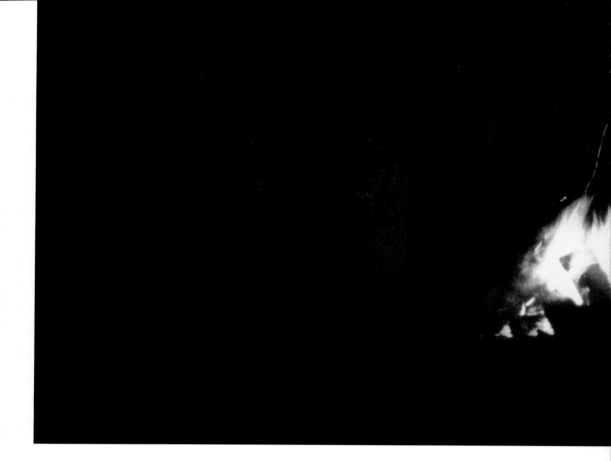

On a cool November evening in Qualla Boundary, North Carolina, Cherokee elder Walker Calhoun leads the stomp dance around the central fire. After the dance, participants gather by the fire and share a meal.

later expansion would have been much less likely. The lands in and around the Navajo Reservation were far from most white settlements in the second half of the 19th century. Thus, few ranchers took advantage of grazing lands in the heart of Dinetah, and by the time they began to, the Navajos were already there with their growing herds of sheep, goats, and horses. By 1900, Navajo sheep herds were estimated at close to a million.

As the Navajo population increased, more lands were added to the original reservation by executive order. Even when the Dawes Severality Act was applied to the Navajos, the result was almost exactly the opposite of what was done to the Cherokees and other native nations. Although allotment was enacted into law in 1887, an agent for the Navajos did not arrive on their isolated reservation until 1905. By then, the act had been modified in a number of ways to make it less harsh on the Indians it affected. None of the territory set aside for the Navajos in 1868 was included in the allotments to individual Navajos that finally did take place. Instead, public lands outside the Navajo reservation, lands into which the growing Navajo popu-

lation had already expanded, were transferred to Navajo ownership.

Things did not always go smoothly between the Navajos and their white neighbors. Occasionally during the gradual Navajo expansion there were serious conflicts. Both Navajos and whites were killed in some of these clashes. The worst threat to peace, however, appears to have been the early resumption by some Navajos of the old practice of livestock raiding off the reservation.

The need to end such raiding has been identified as one of the factors that led to what has been called The Witch Purge of 1878. At that time, 40 Navajo men, some of them prominent figures, were identified as witches and killed. The evil actions of these men, including Muerto de Hombre, one of the signers of the 1868 treaty, were said to be the cause of many problems, from the lack of rain and the death by sorcery of a number of Navajos after the return from Bosque Redondo, to the livestock raids. No one was ever tried for the deaths of those men, but the United States government did step in and prevent any further witch killings.

This drastic traditional response to crisis—not only the raids, but

In the house of her grand-mother in Chinle, Arizona, 12-year-old Sha'nah Dawn Harvey is made ready for the Navajo puberty ceremony called kinaaldá. During the four-day ceremony and rite of passage, she will take on the persona of Changing Woman, the most benevolent of Navajo deities.

On the fourth morning of the kinaaldá, after a night of singing, relatives wash Sha' nah's hair with soap made of yucca roots harvested by her father. With her hair still wet, she will run to the east toward dawn before returning to her family.

the spiritual and psychological turmoil still felt by the Navajos as a result of the Long Walk and the terrible years of imprisonment—appears to have been a true purge. It was followed by an end of the livestock raiding and restored equilibrium.

In the initial decades following the Long Walk, the public perception of the Navajo people gradually changed. Appreciation for the Navajos' reputation as weavers increased, and a new art form—silversmithing—grew rapidly. Silversmithing had been introduced in 1853 by Henry L. Dodge, the much respected Indian agent. His two-year tenure in office was cut short when he was killed by Apaches while hunting. Dodge brought a Mexican blacksmith named George Carter to teach the Navajos the craft of smithing iron and copper. Their ability as metalworkers was proven at Bosque Redondo when engraved metal discs were introduced by the Army as passes to allow Navajos to leave the reservation. Before long, thousands of counterfeit metal passes forged by ingenious Navajos were in circulation.

By the late 1800s, Navajo silversmiths were melting down coins, especially Mexican pesos which were purer silver, to make them into the remarkably beautiful silver jewelry associated with the Navajos to this day. White traders, seeing the market for this new art form, began to import Mexican pesos, supply better tools, and open the market to the tourist industry. Eventually with the help of the Indian Arts and Crafts Board, established in 1935 by the U.S. Department of the Interior, craft guilds were set up on the reservation.

By 1930, the Navajo reservation was close to 12 million acres in size. Goats, horses, burros, nearly 1.5 million sheep and perhaps 200,000 cattle grazed on the land. Observing problems with erosion presumed to be caused by overgrazing, the U.S. government urged the Navajos to voluntarily reduce their livestock. But the government failed to understand the place the animals held in Navajo life. The Navajos regarded them as living beings that were as deeply connected to the land as were the people themselves. The Navajos refused.

Under Commissioner of Indian Affairs John Collier, a drastic program of stock reduction was forced upon the Navajo people in the 1930s. Two-thirds of the sacred animals of the Navajo nation were slaughtered. This was as traumatic for many Navajos as the Long Walk had been. Great numbers of people lost their livelihood, and many lost their will to live. Ironically, the land did not recover but grew worse.

In the book *Between Sacred Mountains,* medicine man George Blue-eyes wrote of this time with great sorrow and explained why stock reduction did not help. "Plants come up only where there are sheep and horses," he said. "Those are the places where it rains. If the ground is hard, when it rains the water just flows. It doesn't soak in. It soaks in only where the sheep walk on it. They walk over their dried manure and mix it with the earth. When it rains, it soaks into the ground with the rain." Another old man, Yellowman's Brother, simply said, "Plants come only from the rain, and the sheep and horses are dressed in rain."

Their words show an understanding of a relatively new theory called "savory grazing," put forward by African scientist Allan Savory, who observed that ranchland in Zimbabwe was much poorer than so-called wild land. The reason was that the large wild herds, which moved often and freely across the land, fertilized the land but did not graze in any one place long enough to kill off the plants as did confined herds of domestic animals. That pattern of free motion across a wide range characterized Navajo herding practices before stock reduction. It appears that Navajo herds at the time of stock reduction were of the right size to exist in balance with the land using traditional practices.

TODAY THE NAVAJOS ARE TRYING TO MAIN-tain traditional values while actively participating in a complex and often contradictory modern world. The last three decades of the 20th century were both a period of growth and optimism, and a time of controversy and confusion for the Navajos. In this period their population doubled, to over 200,000. There were advances in health care and the development of educational institutions that were not merely tolerant of Navajo values, but developed out of them—such as Navajo Community College (later Diné College), which opened in 1973.

One of the reasons for the Long Walk was the belief that there was great wealth hidden in the earth of Dinetah. Removing the Navajos would enable prospectors to enter their lands in search of gold and silver. Such riches were never found during General Carleton's era.

Finally, in the 20th century, the discovery of uranium and coal would bring great economic benefits to the Navajos. By 1980 the Black Mesa mines were the third largest coal producers in the United States.

FOLLOWING PAGES:
Ancient battlements worn by wind and weather, the formations of Monument Valley straddle the Arizona-Utah border on the northern edge of the Navajo Reservation.

185

Sally Sam and her grand-daughter Harriet gather corn from their fields deep in the heart of Canyon de Chelly. Navajo women have a long history as skilled dryland agriculturists and know how to coax crops out of land most farmers would deem too dry for planting.

The mining, while bringing jobs to some Navajos, stirred great controversy. Allegations of misuse of tribal funds damaged the reputations of tribal leaders. There were questions about the health of the Navajo uranium miners. Large-scale strip mining drove people off the land and destroyed the Earth.

Until the Federal Strip Mining law of 1977, the mining companies were not required to do anything to reclaim the land, and they left huge spoil piles. Millions of gallons of water were consumed, and the smoke from the power plants polluted the air and the water. Such injury to the Earth was seen as desecration by many Navajos, who questioned the wisdom of selling their birthright for short-term gains. Those questions are still being asked.

In the area of Big Mountain, where the lands of the Navajos and Hopis come together, strict enforcement of reservation boundaries had been ignored for many years. Navajo and Hopi farmers and herders used the land in common, including the many shrines and sacred places respected by both peoples. Then, in the joint-use area, great deposits of coal were discovered. Would the lucrative mining contracts go to the Hopis or the Navajos? Most of the Hopis and Navajos did not want things changed, but the U.S. Congress decided in 1974 to divide the land.

A line was drawn. Those on the wrong side were told they must leave their former homes by 1986. Only about 120 people of the Hopi Nation (which numbered 8,400) were on the wrong side. However, 9,525 Navajos were told that the land they loved was no longer their own. To the Navajos caught on the wrong side of the line, it was yet another Long Walk. The forced removals were delayed, but it still appeared by the end of the 20th century that the greatest removal of American Indians from their traditional homelands since the end of the 19th century Indian wars would still take place.

Rex Lee Jim is a Navajo poet, writer, and teacher at Diné College. A graduate of Princeton, he wrote the first book of poetry published entirely in the Navajo language. He also co-authored *Living From Livestock*, in which he wrote of how the Navajo Nation was once both wealthy and strong, "because we could live well on our own and usually had enough to trade for things we could not make or grow....Work was hard, but the land fed us. There was even a little bit left over, so there would be feasting at ceremonies, so that people could take time to learn songs and travel among their relatives." Then, as people forgot that the old way meant never using it all, but always leaving that little bit left over, things changed.

"And so," he wrote, "to make a living we look away from our land. We leave home and wander the towns and cities of the West looking for work....We sell the coal, oil, and uranium from our land, even though we know that is a little bit like selling the land itself, because there will never be any more. In the end, if we keep looking away from our land, it will no longer be our home and we will lose it. To hold our place on this land we have to believe that it can give us that little bit left over that will be our share...."

Sally Sam and her family move their sheep through Canyon de Chelly, following a tradition of herding adopted by the Navajos after the Spanish arrived. The sheep are sheared each spring for wool to use in weaving, and their meat is a source of food for ceremonies and for everyday use.

Another way of seeing the world led Rex Lee Jim back home after his education in the East, a way that makes even everyday things of the western world different when seen through Navajo eyes.

Rex proved that to me as we spoke. He took a dollar from his pocket and held it out to me. "If I was going to pay you for something, this is how I would hand you the money," he said. "I would do it with the green side up. That is because the eagle is on this side of the bill." He flipped the dollar over to show me the face of George Washington on the other side. "There is no eagle on this side," he said, "just a man." Then he chuckled. "My grandmother said that you can always trust the eagle, but you cannot always trust the man."

AT THE PARLIAMENT OF WORLD RELIGIONS

held in Chicago in 1993, I asked Navajo Hataałii Hosteen Begay how he came to be a medicine man. "It came to me," he said, and explained how his uncle had been a chanter, but he had never thought to follow that path. He wanted to go into law enforcement. After graduating from the academy, he began work as a policeman, but things kept happening that drew him back to the medicine ways. Finally, after years of indecision, he gave up his career to follow an older way, a path to walk in balance. This was where his heart led him, he said, and there was no way he could refuse.

An event at the Parliament of World Religions made his words more meaningful to me. In a program on religious refugees, displaced Sikhs and Kashmiris and two Navajos were scheduled to talk. The audience of more than 1,500 included a number of Hindus. As the Sikhs began to speak, booing and catcalls rose from the crowd. Soon the atmosphere in the room was charged with violence. It seemed so certain that fighting was about to break out that the security guards locked the doors of the hall to keep the expected riot from spilling out into the rest of the building.

Then the Navajos from Big Mountain took the podium. They began to speak, as softly as the falling of female rain, about this Earth who is mother to us all. They spoke about the sacred nature of life, about the harmony that is also beauty. Angry voices grew quiet and there were tears in the eyes of many who had been on the verge of violence only seconds before. Everyone joined hands and sang "We

Shall Overcome." The Navajo way had drawn peace out of conflict, and found beauty in the midst of suffering.

My own understanding of the Navajo concept of beauty deepened during an autumn visit to Diné College in the heart of the Navajo Nation. A rainbow arced over the administration building as I walked across the campus to Harry Walters's class in Navajo oral history.

Harry introduced himself by his maternal and paternal clans, by the clans of his grandparents, and by the place where he lives. Each student did the same, including two women from Middlebury College in Vermont. With gentle humor, Harry gave his students an overview of the Navajo way of seeing.

"Unlike the Western world, which advocates good, telling people that they should not kill, lie, or steal, then legislates such evils as capital punishment and war," he said, "the Navajo moral construct is more natural and more complex."

He divided the blackboard in half to discuss the two great ceremonial ways. On one side was Beauty Way, on the other Protection Way. Beauty Way contains humor and well-being and the power of innocence. Protection Way is as powerful and potentially dangerous as Bear or Rattlesnake. They are beings who can kill, yet do not do so without warning. Those two Ways balance and complement each other as do Earth and Sky, Woman and Man. Their rules are not man-made but natural, drawn from the four elements of Earth and Water, Air and Sun, in accordance with the continuing cycles of the four seasons, and the four parts of the day, from dawn to sunset.

"Live by these rules," he said, "and you will reach old age and be happy. All of nature has intention to live to old age and be happy." Then he smiled. "When we follow those rules, we walk in beauty."

The Cherokees also have a way of seeing the connection between all things—and all people—a way that has survived against all odds and has much to teach each one of us.

"One of my elders has said that there is one common thread that ties red, white, black and yellow together," Hastings Shade told me. "That is the color red, the blood of all folks. We breathe the same air. Once the breath stops, we're dead. One doesn't die any quicker than the other. We all go back to Mother Earth. Maybe one day we'll come to understand that we're all equal."

FOLLOWING PAGES:
Resembling the arrows of the Hero Twins of Navajo legend, lightning seems to cleanse the land as a thunderstorm rolls across the plains. Navajos on the Long Walk passed through this landscape southwest of Albuquerque, New Mexico.

INDEX

NOTES ON THE AUTHOR

JOSEPH BRUCHAC lives with his wife, Carol, in the Adirondack foothills town of Greenfield Center, New York, where he was raised. His poems, articles, and stories have appeared in numerous publications, including *National Geographic* magazine and *American Poetry Review*. He has been awarded Rockefeller Humanities and NEA Poetry fellowships, and the Lifetime Achievement Award from the Native Writers Circle of the Americas. His most recent books include *Sacajawea*, a novel, and *No Borders*, a collection of poems.

ACKNOWLEDGMENTS

This book would not have been possible without the cooperation of a great many contemporary Native Americans. I'm deeply grateful to Anna Lee and Harry Walters, to Robert and Evelyn Conley, and to Tom Belt and his family for their hospitality and willingness to share so much with me. Sincere thanks to Gayle Ross, who is not only one of America's finest storytellers, but also a passionate voice for the real history of the Aniyunwiya. Shonto Begay and Murv Jacob, two visionary artists whose work can be seen in these pages, also helped guide my journey, as did Freeman Owl, Jerry Wolf, Marijo Moore, Arron Freeland, Tommy Wildcat, and J.T. Garrett. Geary Hobson was one of the first to review this project, and I offer a special thanks to him: *Wado wado*. Thanks also to Native American poets Carroll Arnett and Luci Tapahonso, whose powerful words made me more aware of the Trail of Tears and the Long Walk. To all those not mentioned, including some who prefer to remain unnamed, I offer great thanks. *Ktsi wliwini nidobak*.

FURTHER READING

The Cherokees by Grace Steele Woodward; *Hogans: Navajo Houses and House Songs* by David P. McAllester and Susan W. McAllester; *Navajo Blessingway Singer: The Autobiography of Frank Mitchell*, edited by Charlotte J. Fisbee and David P. McAllester; *The Cherokee People: The Story of the Cherokees from Earliest Origins to Contemporary Times* by Thomas Mails; *The Cherokee* by Theda Purdue; *History, Myths and Sacred Formulas of the Cherokees* by James Mooney; *Sacred Land, Sacred View: Navajo Perceptions of the Four Corners* by Robert S. McPherson; *Fire and the Spirits* by Rennard Strickland; *Indian Removal* by Grant Foreman; *The Book of the Navajo* by Raymond Locke.

TRAILS OF TEARS • PATHS OF BEAUTY
By Joseph Bruchac

Published by the National Geographic Society

John M. Fahey, Jr. *President and Chief Executive Officer*

Gilbert M. Grosvenor *Chairman of the Board*

Nina D. Hoffman *Executive Vice President*

Prepared by the Book Division

William R. Gray *Vice President and Director*

Charles Kogod *Assistant Director*

Barbara A. Payne *Editorial Director and Managing Editor*

Marianne Koszorus *Design Director*

Staff for this Book

Barbara Brownell *Project Editor*

Rebecca Beall Barns *Editor*

Jim Gibson, Gibson Design Associates *Art Director*

John Agnone *Illustrations Editor*

Susan V. Kelly *Researcher*

Carl Mehler *Director of Maps*

XNR Productions *Map Research and Production*

R. Gary Colbert *Production Director*

Richard Wain *Production Project Manager*

Sharon Kocsis Berry *Illustrations Assistant*

Peggy J. Candore *Assistant to the Director*

Robert Witt *Staff Assistant*

Deborah E. Patton *Indexer*

Manufacturing and Quality Management

George V. White *Director*

John T. Dunn *Associate Director*

Vincent P. Ryan Gregory Storer *Managers*

Phillip L. Schlosser *Financial Analyst*

The world's largest nonprofit scientific and educational organization, the National Geographic Society was founded in 1888 "for the increase and diffusion of geographic knowledge." Since then it has supported scientific exploration and spread information to its more than nine million members worldwide.

The National Geographic Society educates and inspires millions every day through magazines, books, television programs, videos, maps and atlases, research grants, the National Geography Bee, teacher workshops, and innovative classroom materials.

The Society is supported through membership dues and income from the sale of its educational products. Members receive NATIONAL GEOGRAPHIC magazine—the Society's official journal—discounts on Society products, and other benefits.

For more information about the National Geographic Society and its educational programs and publications, please call 1-800-NGS-LINE (647-5463), or write to the following address:

National Geographic Society
1145 17th Street N.W.
Washington, D.C. 20036-4688
U.S.A.

Visit the Society's Web site at www.nationalgeographic.com.

Library of Congress Cataloging-in-Publication Data

Bruchac, Joseph, 1942-
    Trails of tears, paths of beauty / Joseph Bruchac.
        p. cm.
    Includes bibliographical references and index.
    ISBN 0-7922-7866-6 (regular) -- ISBN 0-7922-7867-4 (deluxe)
    1. Navajo Indians. 2. Cherokee Indians. I. Title.

E99.N3 B745 2000
979.1'004972--dc21   00-048717